LOVE · MARRIAGE · LOSS · JOURNEYS

JOURNEYS

Also in this series

CHILDHOOD
Edited by Kate Figes

FIRST LOVE
Edited by Paul Bailey

FRIENDSHIP
Edited by Shena Mackay

LOSS
Edited by Elspeth Barker

MARRIAGE
Edited by Elizabeth Jane Howard

JOURNEYS

EDITED BY

Charles Nicholl

J. M. Dent London

First published in Great Britain in 1997
by J. M. Dent

A CIP catalogue record for this book is available
from the British Library.

ISBN 0 460 87932 4

Typeset at The Spartan Press Ltd
Lymington, Hants
Set in 10/11$\frac{1}{2}$pt Photina
Printed in Great Britain by
Clays Ltd, St Ives plc

J. M. Dent

Weidenfeld & Nicolson
The Orion Publishing Group Ltd
Orion House
5 Upper Saint Martin's Lane
London, WC2H 9EA

CONTENTS

INTRODUCTION

♥

Explorers, pilgrims, fugitives, drifters, sun-seekers, back-packers: the list could go on. There are many types of traveller and many types of journey.

Strictly speaking, I suppose, a journey is any movement from one place to another. The longest journey included here is to the moon; the shortest covers a few hundred yards of Dublin pavement as strolled by Leopold Bloom in Joyce's *Ulysses*. The point is not the distance but the movement. 'Our nature lies in movement,' said the philosopher Pascal, 'complete repose is death'. A journey is in this sense an emphatic reminder that one is alive. It is an antidote, if not to death itself, then at least to the *petite mort* of routine. Its footsteps are akin to heartbeats.

In these touristic days, journeys tend to be thought of as an aspect of leisure. They are a desirable commodity to be purchased and consumed: trips, holidays, breaks. The word 'journey' actually tells a rather different story. It connects to an idea of necessity rather than leisure. The word derives from the French *journée*, meaning a day, specifically within the context of day-labour. The traveller is thus, originally, the itinerant job-seeker, the 'journeyman'. The word 'travel', similarly, comes from *travail*, work. In Elizabethan English 'travel' and 'travail' are interchangeable spellings of a single notion of strenuousness.

The archetype of the traveller is the nomad, who travels in order to survive. The medieval journeyman is a version of this; the twentieth-century equivalent is the American hobo, hymned in the songs of Woody Guthrie and of those wandering bluesmen who 'come with the dust and are gone with the wind'.

This is not to downgrade beyond redemption the voluntary traveller or tourist, which is the type of traveller most of us are. (One may swankily refer to oneself as an 'independent traveller', but this broadly means one is a tourist who stays longer and spends less, which is not always good news for one's hosts). There have always been tourists, on tours grand or otherwise, though until this century they were a small, privileged minority. The idea of the traveller as consumer is beautifully caught by the great Jacobean 'leg-stretcher' (as he styled himself) Thomas Coryate, who published an account of his travels in 1611 under the title *Coryate's Crudities*. He means it in the French sense – *crudités*, raw food: these morsels of raw experience which he has 'hastily gobbled up' through half the countries of Europe, and which he now 'digests' and 'disperses' to his readership. (The metaphor inescapably suggests the travel book as a kind of post-prandial fart).

Whatever the mode or motivations of travel, there is nothing like a journey to get people reaching for their pens, if only to write the old lie 'Wish you were here!'. The rich and ancient tradition of travel-writing – the oldest examples here are from Homer (*c.* 850 BC) and Herodotus (died 425 BC) – bears witness to the tonic effect of journeys on our eyes, ears and minds.

Contemporary travel-writing undoubtedly owes its popularity to the prevalence of tourism, yet looks back with implicit nostalgia to a time when travel was all the things that tourism is not: when it was tough and dangerous and full of cultural differences that were scary rather than merely picturesque. As the great explorer von Humboldt put it: 'Perils elevate the poetry of life'. Discomforts and mishaps make better copy than two weeks of Happy Hour cocktails by the pool. (But see Spalding Gray's marvellous take on the search for that elusive 'Perfect Moment' among the palm trees).

At the outer reaches of this are the truly terrible journeys of pioneers and explorers, exemplified here by Cabeza de Vaca's journey of unimaginable privation through northern Mexico in the 1530s, with its wonderful, existential core of revelation: 'we were more than we had thought we were'.

Tourism has also changed the purpose and scope of travel-writing. Its role as pure reportage, as a primary account of places the reader had never been to and was unlikely ever to visit, has been usurped. It is no longer a question of *Joyful News of the New World* – to cite a sixteenth-century travel title – because wherever you are, the place has already been visited and documented. Some of your readers will know it more intimately than you do. This has edged the travel-writer, mostly beneficially, into more subjective and nuanced forms of observation.

For this sort of reason, the distinction between documentary and fictional accounts – both of which are included here – is blurred. All good travel-writing is an act of imagination as much as of data collection; conversely, most of the novelistic journeys here are probably based on personal experience (in the cases of Conrad, Nabokov and Jean Rhys quite certainly so).

This ambiguity seems to me an intrinsic part of travelling: a journey has in itself something of the shape and texture of a story – its beginning and its ending, its cast of characters, its twists and shifts, its curious sense of an underlying pattern whose operation one glimpses from time to time. (Travellers tend to be fatalistic, prone to the omens and coincidences of the road). There is even that liberating sense of rewriting yourself for a while. 'Oh highway!' wrote Walt Whitman, 'you express me better than I can express myself!'

The great Polish foreign correspondent Ryzard Kapuściński speaks of travel-writing as 'literature by foot'. What is written has been 'authenticated' by its being lived: 'You have experienced this event on your own skin, and it is this experience, this feeling along the surface of your skin, that gives your story its coherence.'

This act of witnessing, of being there, is the raw material of travel-writing; a sense of presence – the writer's and consequently the reader's – in the heightened landscape of a journey.

JOURNEYS

IS YOUR JOURNEY REALLY NECESSARY?

ROBERT LOUIS STEVENSON

❧

from *Travels with a Donkey in the Cevennes*

For my part, I travel not to go anywhere, but to go. I travel for travel's sake. The great affair is to move; to feel the needs and hitches of our life more nearly; to come down off this feather-bed of civilization, and find the globe granite underfoot and strewn with cutting flints. Alas, as we get up in life, and are more preoccupied with our affairs, even a holiday is a thing that must be worked for. To hold a pack upon a pack-saddle against a gale out of the freezing north is no high industry, but it is one that serves to occupy and compose the mind. And when the present is so exacting, who can annoy himself about the future?

MATSUO BASHŌ

♥

from *The Narrow Road to the Deep North*

Days and months are travellers of eternity. So are the years that pass by. Those who steer a boat across the sea, or drive a horse over the earth till they succumb to the weight of years, spend every minute of their lives travelling. There are a great number of ancients, too, who died on the road. I myself have been tempted for a long time by the cloud-moving wind – filled with a strong desire to wander.

It was only towards the end of last autumn that I returned from rambling along the coast. I barely had time to sweep the cobwebs from my broken house on the River Sumida before the New Year, but no sooner had the spring mist begun to rise over the field than I wanted to be on the road again to cross the barrier-gate of Shirakawa in due time. The gods seemed to have possessed my soul and turned it inside out, and roadside images seemed to invite me from every corner, so that it was impossible for me to stay idle at home. Even while I was getting ready, mending my torn trousers, tying a new strap to my hat, and applying *moxa* to my legs to strengthen them, I was already dreaming of the full moon rising over the islands of Matsushima. Finally, I sold my house, moving to the cottage of Sampū for a temporary stay. Upon the threshold of my old home, however, I wrote a linked verse of eight pieces and hung it on a wooden pillar. The starting piece was:

Behind this door
Now buried in deep grass,
A different generation will celebrate
The Festival of Dolls.

It was early on the morning of March the twenty-seventh that I took to the road. There was darkness lingering in the sky, and the moon was still visible, though gradually thinning away. The faint shadow of Mount Fuji and the cherry blossoms of Ueno and Yanaka were bidding me a last farewell. My friends had got together the night before, and they all came with me on the boat to keep me company for the first few miles. When we got off the boat at Senju, however, the thought of the three thousand miles before me suddenly filled my heart, and neither the houses of the town nor the faces of my friends could be seen by my tearful eyes except as a vision.

The passing spring,
Birds mourn,
Fishes weep
With tearful eyes.

With this poem to commemorate my departure, I walked forth on my journey, but lingering thoughts made my steps heavy. My friends stood in a line and waved goodbye as long as they could see my back.

HOMER

♥

from *The Odyssey* (Book I)

Sing in me, Muse, and through me tell the story
of that man skilled in all ways of contending,
the wanderer, harried for years on end,
after he plundered the stronghold
on the proud height of Troy.
He saw the townlands
and learned the minds of many distant men,
and weathered many bitter nights and days
in his deep heart at sea, while he fought only
to save his life, to bring his shipmates home.
But not by will nor valour could he save them,
for their own recklessness destroyed them all –
children and fools, they killed and feasted on
the cattle of Lord Hêlios, the Sun,
and he who moves all day through heaven
took from their eyes the dawn of their return.

Of these adventures, Muse, daughter of Zeus,
tell us in our time, lift the great song again.
Begin when all the rest who left behind them
headlong death in battle or at sea
had long ago returned, while he alone still hungered
for home and wife. Her ladyship Kalypso
clung to him in her sea-hollowed caves –
a nymph, immortal and most beautiful,

who craved him for her own.
And when long years and seasons
wheeling brought around that point of time
ordained for him to make his passage homeward,
trials and dangers, even so, attended him
even in Ithaka, near those he loved.
Yet all the gods had pitied Lord Odysseus,
all but Poseidon, raging cold and rough
against the brave king till he came ashore
at last on his own land.

C. P. CAVAFY

'Ithaka'

As you set out for Ithaka
hope your road is a long one,
full of adventure, full of discovery.
Laistrygonians, Cyclops,
angry Poseidon – don't be afraid of them:
you'll never find things like that on your way
as long as you keep your thoughts raised high, ·
as long as a rare excitement
stirs your spirit and your body.
Laistrygonians, Cyclops,
wild Poseidon – you won't encounter them
unless you bring them along inside your soul,
unless your soul sets them up in front of you.

Hope your road is a long one.
May there be many summer mornings when,
with what pleasure, what joy,
you enter harbours you're seeing for the first time;
may you stop at Phoenician trading stations
to buy fine things,
mother of pearl and coral, amber and ebony,
sensual perfume of every kind –
as many sensual perfumes as you can;
and may you visit many Egyptian cities
to learn and go on learning from their scholars.

Keep Ithaka always in your mind.
Arriving there is what you're destined for.
But don't hurry the journey at all.
Better if it lasts for years,
so you're old by the time you reach the island,
wealthy with all you've gained on the way,
not expecting Ithaka to make you rich.

Ithaka gave you the marvellous journey.
Without her you wouldn't have set out.
She has nothing left to give you now.

And if you find her poor, Ithaka won't have fooled you.
Wise as you will have become, so full of experience,
you'll have understood by then what these Ithakas mean.

ANTONIO PIGAFETTA

♥

from *Navigation et Discouvrement*
de la Indie Superieure

I learned that in the city of Seville there was a small *armada* of five ships made ready to perform this long voyage, that is, to discover the islands of Maluco [Molucca] whence the spices come. The Captain-General was a Portuguese gentleman, Fernand de Magaglianes [Magellan], commander of the ship *Santiago*. He had performed several voyages on the Ocean Sea [the Atlantic], in which he showed himself to be a good and honourable man . . . I knew, both by my reading of many books and by the report of many educated and well-informed people, the very great and awful things of the ocean. I decided, with the favour of the Emperor and the Protonotary, to experiment, and to go and see with my own eyes a part of those things. In this way I could satisfy the desire of my lords, and my own desire also; so that it might be said I had performed the said voyage, and seen well with my own eyes the things hereafter written.

LORD BYRON

♥

from *Don Juan*

Juan embark'd – the ship got under way,
   The wind was fair, the water passing rough;
A devil of a sea rolls in that bay,
   As I, who've cross'd it oft, know well enough;
And, standing upon deck, the dashing spray
   Flies in one's face, and makes it weather-tough:
And there he stood to take, and take again,
His first – perhaps his last – farewell of Spain.

I can't but say it is an awkward sight
   To see one's native land receding through
The growing waters; it unmans one quite,
   Especially when life is rather new:
I recollect Great Britain's coast looks white,
   But almost every other country's blue,
When gazing on them, mystified by distance,
We enter on our nautical existence.

So Juan stood, bewilder'd on the deck:
   The wind sung, cordage strain'd, and sailors swore,
And the ship creak'd, the town became a speck,
   From which away so fair and fast they bore.
The best of remedies is a beef-steak
   Against sea-sickness, try it, sir, before
You sneer, and I assure you this is true,
For I have found it answer – so may you.

Don Juan stood, and, gazing from the stern,
    Beheld his native Spain receding far:
First partings form a lesson hard to learn,
    Even nations feel this when they go to war;
There is a sort of unexprest concern,
    A kind of shock that sets one's heart ajar:
At leaving even the most unpleasant people
And places, one keeps looking at the steeple.

But Juan had got many things to leave,
    His mother, and a mistress, and no wife,
So that he had much better cause to grieve
    Than many persons more advanced in life;
And if we now and then a sigh must heave
    At quitting even those we quit in strife,
No doubt we weep for those the heart endears –
That is, till deeper griefs congeal our tears.

So Juan wept, as wept the captive Jews
    By Babel's waters, still remembering Sion:
I'd weep, – but mine is not a weeping Muse,
    And such light griefs are not a thing to die on;
Young men should travel, if but to amuse
    Themselves; and the next time their servants tie on
Behind their carriage their new portmanteau,
Perhaps it may be lined with this my canto.

And Juan wept, and much he sigh'd and thought,
    While his salt tears dropp'd into the salt sea,
'Sweets to the sweet'; (I like so much to quote;
    You must excuse this extract, – 'tis where she,
The Queen of Denmark, for Ophelia brought
    Flowers to the grave;) and, sobbing often, he
Reflected on his present situation,
And seriously resolved on reformation.

11

'Farewell, my Spain! a long farewell!' he cried,
    'Perhaps I may revisit thee no more,
But die, as many an exiled heart hath died,
    Of its own thirst to see again thy shore:
Farewell, where Guadalquivir's waters glide!
    Farewell, my mother! and, since all is o'er,
Farewell, too, dearest Julia! – (here he drew
Her letter out again, and read it through.)

'And oh! if e'er I should forget, I swear –
    But that's impossible, and cannot be –
Sooner shall this blue ocean melt to air,
    Sooner shall earth resolve itself to sea,
Than I resign thine image, oh, my fair!
    Or think of anything excepting thee;
A mind diseased no remedy can physic –
(Here the ship gave a lurch, and he grew sea-sick.)

'Sooner shall heaven kiss earth – (here he fell sicker)
    Oh Julia! what is every other woe? –
(For God's sake let me have a glass of liquor;
    Pedro, Battista, help me down below.)
Julia, my love! – (you rascal, Pedro, quicker) –
    Oh, Julia! – (this curst vessel pitches so) –
Beloved Julia, hear me still beseeching!'
    (Here he grew inarticulate with retching.)

He felt that chilling heaviness of heart,
    Or rather stomach, which, alas! attends,
Beyond the best apothecary's art,
    The loss of love, the treachery of friends,
Or death of those we dote on, when a part
    Of us dies with them as each fond hope ends:
No doubt he would have been much more pathetic,
But the sea acted as a strong emetic.

LAURENCE STERNE

❦

from *A Sentimental Journey Through France and Italy*

– They order, said I, this matter better in France –
– You have been in France? said my gentleman, turning quick upon me with the most civil triumph in the world. – Strange! quoth I, debating the matter with myself, That one and twenty miles sailing, for 'tis absolutely no further from Dover to Calais, should give a man these rights – I'll look into them: so giving up the argument – I went straight to my lodgings, put up half a dozen shirts and a black pair of silk breeches – 'the coat I have on, said I, looking at the sleeve, will do' – took a place in the Dover stage; and the packet sailing at nine the next morning – by three I had got sat down to my dinner upon a fricasee'd chicken, so incontestably in France, that had I died that night of an indigestion, the whole world could not have suspended the effects of the *Droits d'aubaine** – my shirts, and black pair of silk breeches – portmanteau and all must have gone to the king of France – even the little picture which I have so long worn, and so often have told thee, Eliza, I would carry with me into my grave, would have been torn from my neck. – Ungenerous! – to seize upon the wreck of an unwary

---

* All the effects of strangers (Swiss and Scotch excepted) dying in France, are seized by virtue of this law, though the heir be upon the spot – the profit of these contingencies being farmed, there is no redress.

passenger, whom your subjects had beckoned to their coast – by heaven! SIRE, it is not well done; and much does it grieve me, 'tis the monarch of a people so civilized and courteous, and so renowned for sentiment and fine feelings, that I have to reason with ——

But I have scarce set foot in your dominions –

DANTE

from *The Divine Comedy*

Midway on our life's journey, I found myself
   In dark woods, the right road lost. To tell
   About those woods is hard – so tangled and rough

And savage that thinking of it now, I feel
   The old fear stirring: death is hardly more bitter.
   And yet, to treat the good I found there as well

I'll tell what I saw, though how I came to enter
   I cannot well say, being so full of sleep
   Whatever moment it was I began to blunder

Off the true path. But when I came to stop
   Below a hill that marked one end of the valley
   That had pierced my heart with terror, I looked up

Toward the crest and saw its shoulders already
   Mantled in rays of that bright planet that shows
   The road to everyone, whatever our journey.

Then I could feel the terror begin to ease
   That churned in my heart's lake all through the night.
   As one still panting, ashore from dangerous seas,

Looks back at the deep he has escaped, my thought
    Returned, still fleeing, to regard that grim defile
    That never left any alive who stayed in it.

After I had rested my weary body awhile
    I started again across the wilderness,
    My left foot always lower on the hill,

And suddenly – a leopard, near the place
    The way grew steep: lithe, spotted, quick of foot.
    Blocking the path, she stayed before my face

And more than once she made me turn about
    To go back down. It was early morning still,
    The fair sun rising with the stars attending it

As when Divine Love set those beautiful
    Lights into motion at creation's dawn,
    And the time of day and season combined to fill

My heart with hope of that beast with festive skin –
    But not so much that the next sight wasn't fearful:
    A lion came at me, his head high as he ran,

Roaring with hunger so the air appeared to tremble.
    Then a grim she-wolf – whose leanness seemed to
        compress
    All the world's cravings, that had made miserable

Such multitudes; she put such heaviness
    Into my spirit, I lost hope of the crest.
    Like someone eager to win, who tested by loss

Surrenders to gloom and weeps, so did that beast
    Make me feel, as hurrying toward me at a lope
    She forced me back toward where the sun is lost.

THOMAS RHYMER

And see not ye that braid braid road
That lies across yon lilly leven?
That is the path of wickedness
Tho some call it the road to heaven . . .

HUNTER S. THOMPSON

♪

from *Fear and Loathing in Las Vegas*

We were somewhere around Barstow on the edge of the desert when the drugs began to take hold. I remember saying something like 'I feel a bit lightheaded; maybe you should drive . . .' And suddenly there was a terrible roar all around us and the sky was full of what looked like huge bats, all swooping and screeching and diving around the car, which was going about a hundred miles an hour with the top down to Las Vegas. And a voice was screaming: 'Holy Jesus! What are these goddamn animals?'

Then it was quiet again. My attorney had taken his shirt off and was pouring beer on his chest, to facilitate the tanning process. 'What the hell are you yelling about?' he muttered, staring up at the sun with his eyes closed and covered with wrap-around Spanish sunglasses. 'Never mind,' I said. 'It's your turn to drive.' I hit the brakes and aimed the Great Red Shark toward the shoulder of the highway. No point mentioning those bats, I thought. The poor bastard will see them soon enough.

It was almost noon, and we still had more than a hundred miles to go. They would be tough miles. Very soon, I knew, we would both be completely twisted. But there was no going back, and no time to rest. We would have to ride it out. Press registration for the fabulous Mint 400 was already underway, and we had to get there by four to claim our sound-proof suite. A fashionable sporting magazine in

New York had taken care of the reservations, along with this huge red Chevy convertible we'd just rented off a lot on the Sunset Strip . . . and I was, after all, a professional journalist; so I had an obligation to *cover the story*, for good or ill.

The sporting editors had also given me $300 in cash, most of which was already spent on extremely dangerous drugs. The trunk of the car looked like a mobile police narcotics lab. We had two bags of grass, seventy-five pellets of mescaline, five sheets of high-powered blotter acid, a salt shaker half full of cocaine, and a whole galaxy of multi-coloured uppers, downers, screamers, laughers . . . and also a quart of tequila, a quart of rum, a case of Budweiser, a pint of raw ether and two dozen amyls.

All this had been rounded up the night before, in a frenzy of high-speed driving all over Los Angeles County – from Topanga to Watts, we picked up everything we could get our hands on. Not that we *needed* all that for the trip, but once you get locked into a serious drug collection, the tendency is to push it as far as you can.

The only thing that really worried me was the ether. There is nothing in the world more helpless and irresponsible and depraved than a man in the depths of an ether binge. And I knew we'd get into that rotten stuff pretty soon. Probably at the next gas station. We had sampled almost everything else, and now – yes, it was time for a long snort of ether. And then do the next hundred miles in a horrible, slobbering sort of spastic stupor. The only way to keep alert on ether is to do up a lot of amyls – not all at once, but steadily, just enough to maintain the focus at ninety miles an hour through Barstow.

'Man, this is the way to travel,' said my attorney. He leaned over to turn the volume up on the radio, humming along with the rhythm section and kind of moaning the words: 'One toke over the line, Sweet Jesus . . . One toke over the line . . .'

One toke? You poor fool! Wait till you see those goddamn bats. I could barely hear the radio . . . slumped over on the far side of the seat, grappling with a tape recorder turned all the way up on 'Sympathy for the Devil'. That was the only tape we had, so we played it constantly, over and over, as a kind of demented counterpoint to the radio. And also to maintain our rhythm on the road. A constant speed is good for gas mileage – and for some reason that seemed important at the time. Indeed. On a trip like this one *must* be careful about gas consumption. Avoid those quick bursts of acceleration that drag blood to the back of the brain.

My attorney saw the hitchhiker long before I did. 'Let's give this boy a lift,' he said, and before I could mount any argument he was stopped and this poor Okie kid was running up to the car with a big grin on his face saying, 'Hot damn! I never rode in a convertible before!'

'Is that right?' I said. 'Well, I guess you're about ready eh?'

The kid nodded eagerly as we roared off.

'We're your friends,' said my attorney. 'We're not like the others.'

O Christ, I thought, he's gone around the bend. 'No more of that talk,' I said sharply. 'Or I'll put the leeches on you.' He grinned, seeming to understand. Luckily, the noise in the car was so awful – between the wind and the radio and the tape machine – that the kid in the back seat couldn't hear a word we were saying. Or could he?

How long can we *maintain*? I wondered. How long before one of us starts raving and jabbering at this boy? What will he think then? This same lonely desert was the last known home of the Manson family. Will he make that grim connection when my attorney starts screaming about bats and huge manta rays coming down on the car? If so – well, we'll just have to cut his head off and bury him somewhere. Because it goes without saying that we can't turn him loose. He'll report us at once to some kind of outback nazi law enforcement agency, and they'll run us down like dogs.

Jesus! did I *say* that? Or just think it? Was I talking? Did they hear me? I glanced over at my attorney, but he seemed oblivious – watching the road, driving our Great Red Shark along at a hundred and ten or so. There was no sound from the back seat.

Maybe I'd better have a chat with this boy, I thought. Perhaps if I *explain* things, he'll rest easy.

Of course. I leaned around in the seat and gave him a fine big smile . . . admiring the shape of his skull.

'By the way,' I said. 'There's one thing you should probably understand.'

He stared at me, not blinking. Was he gritting his teeth?

'Can you *hear* me?' I yelled.

He nodded.

'That's good,' I said. 'Because I want you to know that we're on our way to Las Vegas to find the American Dream.' I smiled. 'That's why we rented this car. It was the only way to do it. Can you grasp that?'

He nodded again, but his eyes were nervous.

'I want you to have all the background,' I said. 'Because this is a very ominous assignment – with overtones of extreme personal danger . . . Hell, I forgot all about this beer; you want one?'

He shook his head.

'How about some ether?' I said.

'What?'

'Never mind. Let's get right to the heart of this thing. You see, about twenty-four hours ago we were sitting in the Polo Lounge of the Beverly Hills Hotel – in the patio section, of course – and we were just sitting there under a palm tree when this uniformed dwarf came up to me with a pink telephone and said, "This must be the call you've been waiting for all this time, sir." '

I laughed and ripped open a beer can that foamed all over the back seat while I kept talking. 'And you know? He was right! I'd been *expecting* that call, but I didn't know who it would come from. Do you follow me?'

The boy's face was a mask of pure fear and bewilderment.

I blundered on: 'I want you to understand that this man at the wheel is my *attorney*! He's not just some dingbat I found on the Strip. Shit, *look* at him! He doesn't look like you or me, right? That's because he's a foreigner. I think he's probably Samoan. But it doesn't matter, does it? Are you prejudiced?'

'Oh, hell *no*!' he blurted.

'I didn't think so,' I said. 'Because in spite of his race, this man is extremely valuable to me.' I glanced over at my attorney, but his mind was somewhere else.

I whacked the back of the driver's seat with my fist. 'This is *important*, goddamnit! This is a *true story*!' The car swerved sickeningly, then straightened out. 'Keep your hands off my fucking neck!' my attorney screamed. The kid in the back looked like he was ready to jump right out of the car and take his chances.

Our vibrations were getting nasty – but why? I was puzzled, frustrated. Was there no communication in this car? Had we deteriorated to the level of *dumb beasts*?

FANNY KEMBLE

Aboard Stephenson's 'Rocket', April 1830

. . . We were introduced to the little engine which was to drag us along the rails . . . This snorting little animal, which I felt rather inclined to pat, was then harnessed to our carriage, and, Mr Stephenson having taken me on the bench of the engine with him, we started at about ten miles an hour. The steam-horse being ill-adapted for going up and down hill, the road was kept at a certain level, and appeared sometimes to sink below the surface of the earth, and sometimes to rise above it. Almost at starting it was cut through the solid rock, which formed a wall on either side of it, about sixty feet high. You can't imagine how strange it seemed to be journeying on thus, without any visible cause of progress other than the magical machine, with its flying white breath and rhythmical, unvarying pace . . .

We had now come fifteen miles, and stopped where the road traversed a wide and deep valley. Stephenson made me alight and led me down to the bottom of this ravine, over which, in order to keep his road level, he has thrown a magnificent viaduct of nine arches, the middle one of which is seventy feet high, through which we saw the whole of this beautiful little valley . . . We then rejoined the rest of the party, and the engine having received its supply of water, the carriage was placed behind it, for it cannot turn, and was set off at its utmost speed, thirty-five miles an hour, swifter than a bird flies (for they tried the experiment with a snipe). You cannot conceive what that sensation of cutting the air was; the motion is as smooth as possible, too. I could either have read or written.

SAMUEL JOHNSON

from Boswell's *Life of Johnson*, 19 September 1777

If . . . I had no duties, and no reference to futurity, I would spend my life in driving briskly in a post-chaise with a pretty woman.

CHARLES DICKENS

♥

from *Dombey and Son*

Gathered up moodily in a corner of the carriage, and only intent on going fast – except when he stood up, for a mile together, and looked back; which he would do whenever there was a piece of open country – he went on, still postponing thought indefinitely, and still always tormented with thinking to no purpose.

Shame, disappointment, and discomfiture gnawed at his heart; a constant apprehension of being overtaken, or met – for he was groundlessly afraid even of travellers who came towards him by the way he was going – oppressed him heavily. The same intolerable awe and dread that had come upon him in the night, returned unweakened in the day. The monotonous ringing of the bells and tramping of the horses; the monotony of his anxiety, and useless rage; the monotonous wheel of fear, regret, and passion, he kept turning round and round; made the journey like a vision, in which nothing was quite real but his own torment.

It was a vision of long roads; that stretched away to an horizon, always receding and never gained; of ill-paved towns, up hill and down, where faces came to dark doors and ill-glazed windows, and where rows of mud-bespattered cows and oxen were tied up for sale in the long narrow streets, butting and lowing, and receiving blows on their blunt heads from bludgeons that might have beaten them in; of bridges, crosses, churches, postyards, new horses being put in against their wills, and the horses of the last stage reeking, panting, and laying their drooping heads together dolefully at stable doors; of little cemeteries with black crosses settled sideways in the graves; and withered wreaths upon them dropping away; again of long, long roads, dragging themselves out, up hill and down, to the treacherous horizon.

Of morning, noon and sunset, night, and the rising of an early moon. Of long roads temporarily left behind, and a rough pavement reached; of battering and clattering over it, and looking up, among house-roofs, at a great church-tower, of getting out and eating hastily, and drinking draughts of wine that had no cheering influence; of coming forth afoot, among a host of beggars – blind men with quivering eyelids, led by old women holding candles to their faces; idiot girls; the lame, the epileptic, and the palsied – of passing through the clamour, and looking from his seat at the upturned countenances and outstretched hands, with a hurried dread of recognizing some pursuer pressing forward – of galloping away again, upon the long, long road, gathered up, dull and stunned, in his corner, or rising to see where the moon shone faintly on a patch of the same endless road miles away, or looking back to see who followed.

Of never sleeping, but sometimes dozing with unclosed eyes, and springing up with a start, and a reply aloud to an imaginary voice. Of cursing himself for being there, for having fled, for having let her go, for not having confronted and defied him. Of having a deadly quarrel with the whole world, but chiefly with himself. Of blighting everything with his black mood as he was carried on and away.

It was a fevered vision of things past and present all confounded together, of his life and journey blended into one. Of being madly hurried somewhere, whither he must go. Of old scenes starting up among the novelties through which he travelled. Of musing and brooding over what was past and distant, and seeming to take no notice of the actual

27

objects he encountered, but with a wearisome exhausting consciousness of being bewildered by them, and having their images all crowded in his hot brain after they were gone.

A vision of change upon change, and still the same monotony of bells and wheels, and horses' feet, and no rest. Of town and country, postyards, horses, drivers, hill and valley, light and darkness, road and pavement, height and hollow, wet weather and dry, and still the same monotony of bells and wheels, and horses' feet, and no rest. A vision of tending on at last, towards the distant capital, by busier roads, and sweeping round, by old cathedrals, and dashing through small towns and villages, less thinly scattered on the road than formerly, and sitting shrouded in his corner, with his cloak up to his face, as people passing by looked at him.

Of rolling on and on, always postponing thought, and always racked with thinking; of being unable to reckon up the hours he had been upon the road, or to comprehend the points of time and place in his journey. Of being parched and giddy, and half mad. Of pressing on, in spite of all, as if he could not stop, and coming into Paris, where the turbid river held its swift course undisturbed, between two brawling streams of life and motion.

JOHN DONNE

from 'Verse-letter to Sir Henry Wotton'

Be thou thine own home, and in thy self dwell;
Inn anywhere, continuance maketh hell.
And seeing the snail, which everywhere doth roam,
Carrying his own house still, still is at home,
Follow (for he is easy pac'd) this snail,
Be thine own palace, or the world's thy gale.
And in the world's sea do not, like cork, sleep
Upon the water's face; nor in the deep
Sink like a lead without a line; but as
Fishes glide, leaving no print where they pass,
Nor making sound, so closely thy course go,
Let men dispute whether thou breathe or no.

GEORGE HERBERT

from 'The Collar'

I struck the board, and cry'd, No more.
                    I will abroad.
          What? shall I ever sigh and pine?
My lines and life are free; free as the road,
Loose as the wind, as large as store.

ARTHUR RIMBAUD

from 'Childhood'

I am the tramper of the highway, through the dwarfish woods. The whispering of the sluices covers my steps. For a long time I can see the melancholy gold wash of sunset.

I could be a child, abandoned on the wharf, setting off for the high seas, or a farm lad walking a lane whose top touches the sky.

The trails are hard. The slopes are covered with broom. The air is quite still. How far away the birds and the brooks are! This must surely be the end of the world I'm coming up to.

I CHING

Fire on the mountain:
the image of the wanderer

KENNETH ALLSOP

❦

'The Hobo'

The shock-trooper of the American expansion, the man with bed-roll on back who free-lanced beyond the community redoubts, building the canals and roads and rights-of-way, spiking rails, felling timber, drilling oil, digging mines, fencing prairie, harvesting wheat, was the hobo.

He was homeless and unmarried. He freeloaded on the freight trains whose tracks he laid and whose tunnels he blasted. He lived in bunk houses or tents or jungle camps or city flophouses. He was a marginal, alienated man, capriciously used and discarded by a callous but dynamic system, yet he was proud of the mode he devised out of an imperative mobility. He was a unique and indigenous American product.

He formed the moving labour corps which followed the advancing line across the continent, and he answered the market demand for manpower where none existed in the new, rough country. He staked down with his hammer the provisional frontier.

In one of his aspects he was the Ancient Mariner of this oceanic land, the albatross of failure hung about his neck. In his militant political role, as a Wobbly, a red card carrier of the Industrial Workers of the World, he was 'half industrial slave, half vagabond adventurer . . . the *francs tireurs* of the class struggle'.

He often got drunk and squandered the money he had sweated for. He was a wild and recalcitrant wayfarer, bothersome to the settled citizen who disapproved of him and perhaps secretly envied him. Out there in the offing he developed his own distinct life and philosophy: tough, reckless, radical, sardonic. A romantic essence of the hobo's style has impregnated American song, literature and outlook.

Considering the degree to which it has, he has been surprisingly neglected as a subject of study. Information about him is scattered, piecemeal, throughout seventy years of autobiography, fiction, poetry, folk song, sociology and economic surveys, yet his genesis was really much earlier, and few attempts have been made, and none in recent years, to examine his origins, the type and the influence of the wandering worker in America.

His habitat has changed but his habits have not, not all that much. For he is still there, a sundry part of the tidal restlessness of American life; and the hobo idea, or impulse, is even more widely present, the eagerly seized inheritance of the young of an urbanized society in which the hobo is theoretically obsolete . . .

WOODY GUTHRIE

'Hard Travellin''

I been hittin' some hard travellin', I thought you knowed.
I been hittin' some hard travellin', way down the road.
I been hittin' some hard travellin', hard ramblin', hard
    gamblin'.
I been hittin' some hard travellin', Lord.

I been ridin' them fast rattlers, I thought you knowed.
I been ridin' them flat wheelers, way down the road.
I been ridin' those dead enders, blind passengers, kickin' up
    cinders.
I been hittin' some hard travellin', Lord . . .

I been layin' in a hard-rock jail, I thought you knowed.
I been layin' out ninety days, way down the road.
Mean old judge, he says to me,
'It's ninety days for vagrancy.'
An' I been hittin' some hard travellin', Lord.

Well, I been hittin' some hard harvestin', I thought you
    knowed.
North Dakota to Kansas City, way down the road.
Cuttin' that wheat and a-stackin' that hay,
Tryin' to make about a dollar a day.
I been hittin' some hard travellin', Lord.

I been walkin' that Lincoln Highway, I thought you
knowed.
I been hittin' that Sixty-six, way down the road.
Heavy load and a worried mind.
Lookin' for a woman that's hard to find.
An' I been hittin' some hard travellin', Lord.

JACK KEROUAC

♥

from *On the Road*

The tourists insisted on driving the car the rest of the way to Denver. Okay, we didn't care. We sat in the back and talked. But they got too tired in the morning and Dean took the wheel in the eastern Colorado desert at Craig. We had spent almost the entire night crawling cautiously over Strawberry Pass in Utah and lost a lot of time. They went to sleep. Dean headed pellmell for the mighty wall of Berthoud Pass that stood a hundred miles ahead on the roof of the world, a tremendous Gibraltarian door shrouded in clouds. He took Berthoud Pass like a June bug – same as at Tehachapi, cutting off the motor and floating it, passing everybody and never halting the rhythmic advance that the mountains themselves intended, till we overlooked the great hot plain of Denver again – and Dean was home.

It was with a great deal of silly relief that these people let us off the car at the corner of 27th and Federal. Our battered suitcases were piled on the sidewalk again; we had longer ways to go. But no matter, the road is life.

'Tom o' Bedlam's Song'

From the hag and hungry goblin
That into rags would rend ye,
   The spirits that stand
   By the naked man
In the book of Moons, defend ye,
That of your five sound senses
You never be forsaken,
   Nor wander from
   Yourselves with Tom
Abroad to beg your bacon.

When I short have shorn my sow's face
And swigged my horny barrel,
   In an oaken inn
   I pound my skin
As a suit of gilt apparel.
While I sing, 'Any food, any feeding,
Feeding, drink, or clothing?
   Come, dame or maid,
   Be not afraid,
Poor Tom will injure nothing.'

Of thirty bare years have I
Twice twenty been enraged,
   And of forty been

Three times fifteen
In durance soundly caged,
On the lordly lofts of Bedlam,
With stubble soft and dainty,
    Brave bracelets strong,
    Sweet whips, ding-dong,
With wholesome hunger plenty.

The Moon's my constant mistress
And the lonely owl my marrow.
    The flaming drake
    And the nightcrow make
Me music to my sorrow.
I slept not since the Conquest,
Till then I never waked,
    Till the roguish fay
    Of love where I lay
Me found and stript me naked.

I know more than Apollo,
For oft, when he lies sleeping,
    I see the stars
    At bloody wars
And the wounded welkin weeping,
The moon embrace her shepherd,
And the queen of love her warrior,
    While the first doth horn
    The star of the morn,
And the next the heavenly farrier.

The gypsies Snap and Pedro
Are none of Tom's comradoes;
    The punk I scorn
    And the cutpurse sworn,
And the roaring-boys' bravadoes;
The meek, the white, the gentle
Me handle, touch, and spare not,

But those that cross
   Tom Rhinoceros
Do what the panther dare not.

With an host of furious fancies,
Whereof I am commander,
   With a burning spear
   And a horse of air
To the wilderness I wander;
By a knight of ghosts and shadows
I summoned am to tourney
   Ten leagues beyond
   The wide world's end –
Methinks it is no journey.

I'll bark against the dogstar,
And crow away the morning;
   I'll chase the moon
   Till it be noon,
And I'll make her leave her horning.
But I will find bonny Maud, merry mad Maud,
I'll seek whate'er betides her,
   And I will love
   Beneath or above
That dirty earth that hides her.

RYSZARD KAPUŚCIŃSKI

The Forest of Things

Sometimes in describing what I do, I resort to the Latin phrase, *silva rerum*: the forest of things. That's my subject: the forest of things, as I've seen it, living and travelling in it. To capture the world you have to penetrate it as completely as possible ... The story is the beginning. It is half the achievement. But it is not complete until you, as the writer, become part of it. As a writer, you have experienced this event on your own skin, and it is this experience, this feeling along the surface of your skin, that gives your story its coherence ... It is terribly important to have what I write authenticated by its being lived. You could call it, I suppose, personal reportage, because the author is always present. I sometimes call it literature by foot ...

PARACELSUS

from *Sieben Defensiones*

He who wishes to explore Nature must tread her books with his feet. Writing is learnt from letters, but Nature from land to land. One land, one page. Thus is the *Codex Naturae*, thus must its leaves be turned.

VLADIMIR NABOKOV

from *Lolita*

It was then that began our extensive travels all over the States. To any other type of tourist accommodation I soon grew to prefer the Functional Motel – clean, neat, safe nooks, ideal places for sleep, argument, reconciliation, insatiable illicit love. At first, in my dread of arousing suspicion, I would eagerly pay for both sections of one double unit, each containing a double bed. I wondered what type of foursome this arrangement was ever intended for, since only a pharisaic parody of privacy could be attained by means of the incomplete partition dividing the cabin or room into two communicating love nests. By and by, the very possibilities that such honest promiscuity suggested (two young couples merrily swapping mates or a child shamming sleep to ear-witness primal sonorities) made me bolder, and every now and then I would take a bed-and-cot or twin-bed cabin, a prison cell of paradise, with yellow window shades pulled down to create a morning illusion of Venice and sunshine when actually it was Pennsylvania and rain.

We came to know – *nous connûmes*, to use a Flaubertian intonation – the stone cottages under enormous Chateaubriandesque trees, the brick unit, the adobe unit, the stucco court, on what the Tour Book of the Automobile Association describes as 'shaded' or 'spacious' or 'landscaped' grounds. The log kind, finished in knotty pine, reminded Lo, by its golden-brown glaze, of fried-chicken bones. We held in contempt the plain whitewashed clapboard Kabins, with their faint sewerish smell or some other gloomy self-conscious stench and nothing to boast of (except 'good beds'), and an unsmiling landlady always prepared to have her gift (' . . . well, I could give you . . .') turned down.

Nous connûmes (this is royal fun) the would-be enticements of their repetitious names – all those Sunset Motels, U-Beam Cottages, Hillcrest Courts, Pine View Courts, Mountain View Courts, Skyline Courts, Park Plaza Courts, Green Acres, Mac's Courts. There was sometimes a special line in the write-up, such as 'Children welcome, pets allowed' (*You* are welcome, *you* are allowed). The baths were mostly tiled showers, with an endless variety of spouting mechanisms, but with one definitely non-Laodicean characteristic in common, a propensity, while in use, to turn instantly beastly hot or blindingly cold upon you, depending on whether your neighbour turned on his cold or his hot to deprive you of a necessary complement in the shower you had so carefully blended. Some motels had instructions pasted above the toilet (on whose tank the towels were unhygienically heaped) asking guests not to throw into its bowl garbage, beer cans, cartons, stillborn babies; others had special notices under glass, such as Things to Do (Riding: *You will often see riders coming down Main Street on their way back from a romantic moonlight ride.* 'Often at 3 a.m.,' sneered unromantic Lo).

Nous connûmes the various types of motor court operators, the reformed criminal, the retired teacher and the business flop, among the males; and the motherly, pseudo-ladylike and madamic variants among the females. And sometimes trains would cry in the monstrously hot and humid night with heartrending and ominous plangency, mingling power and hysteria in one desperate scream . . .

Immediately upon arrival at one of the plainer motor courts which became our habitual haunts, she would set

44

the electric fan a-whirr, or induce me to drop a quarter into the radio, or she would read all the signs and inquire with a whine why she could not go riding up some advertised trail or swimming in that local pool of warm mineral water. Most often, in the slouching, bored way she cultivated, Lo would fall prostrate and abominably desirable into a red spring chair, or a green chaise longue, or a steamer chair of striped canvas with footrest and canopy, or a sling chair, or any other lawn chair under a garden umbrella on the patio, and it would take hours of blandishments, threats and promises to make her lend me for a few seconds her brown limbs in the seclusion of the five-dollar room before undertaking anything she might prefer to my poor joy . . .

By putting the geography of the United States into motion, I did my best for hours on end to give her the impression of 'going places', of rolling on to some definite destination, to some unusual delight. I have never seen such smooth amiable roads as those that now radiated before us, across the crazy quilt of forty-eight states. Voraciously we consumed those long highways, in rapt silence we glided over their glossy black dance floors. Not only had Lo no eye for scenery but she furiously resented my calling her attention to this or that enchanting detail of landscape; which I myself learned to discern only after being exposed for quite a time to the delicate beauty ever present in the margin of our undeserving journey . . .

Beyond the tilled plain, beyond the toy roofs, there would be a slow suffusion of inutile loveliness, a low sun in a platinum haze with a warm, peeled-peach tinge pervading the upper edge of a two-dimensional, dove-grey cloud fusing with the distant amorous mist. There might be a line of spaced trees silhouetted against the horizon, and hot still noons above a wilderness of clover, and Claude Lorrain clouds inscribed remotely into misty azure with only their cumulus part conspicuous against the neutral swoon of the background. Or again, it might be a stern El Greco horizon, pregnant with inky rain, and a passing glimpse of some mummy-necked farmer, and all around alternating strips of quicksilverish water and harsh green corn, the whole arrangement opening like a fan, somewhere in Kansas.

Now and then, in the vastness of those plains, huge trees would advance toward us to cluster self-consciously by the roadside and provide a bit of humanitarian shade above a picnic table, with sun flecks, flattened paper cups, samaras and discarded ice-cream sticks littering the brown ground. A great user of roadside facilities, my unfastidious Lo would be charmed by toilet signs – Guys-Gals, John-Jane, Jack-Jill and even Buck's-Doe's; while lost in an artist's dream, I would stare at the honest brightness of the gasoline para-phernalia against the splendid green of oaks, or at a distant hill scrambling out – scarred but still untamed – from the wilderness of agriculture that was trying to swallow it.

At night, tall trucks studded with coloured lights, like dreadful giant Christmas trees, loomed in the darkness and thundered by the belated little sedan. And again next day a thinly populated sky, losing its blue to the heat, would melt overhead, and Lo would clamour for a drink, and her cheeks would hollow vigorously over the straw, and the car inside would be a furnace when we got in again, and the road shimmered ahead, with a remote car changing its shape mirage-like in the surface glare, and seeming to hang for a moment, old-fashionedly square and high, in the hot haze.

ALFRED WATKINS

from *The Old Straight Track*

In noting place-names on the straight track it gradually becomes evident that the local characteristics of the spot are often a minor influence; the track itself, its character, the men who made it, who came along it, or the goods they carried giving names to places all along the line . . . It may be that all the first straight ways were made for trading, for man must have very early had need for necessities, such as salt, flint, and (later) metals, not found in his own district.

One such type of roads – the salt way – has left place-names so loudly proclaiming the meaning that observers have long recognized it; and Alles in his *Folk Lore of Worcestershire* attempts to follow several leading from Droitwich. He mentions a number of field names, Sale (four of these), Salt Moor, Salt Way (piece, barn and coppice). Salt place-names abound: Saltley, Salford, Sale (Cheshire), Saltash. Probably they originated in Romano-British times, for philologists trace our word 'salary' to the *salarium* of the Roman soldier, being an allowance for the purchase of salt; and an inefficient salaried man is even now said to be 'not worth his salt'. It seems, therefore, plain that when the salary was exchanged with the trader for salt the transaction came to be called a sale, and as will be seen when we come to the 'chip' and 'cheap' places, it was not the only instance of the evolution of trading terms from early products.

But there were at least two other types of names, probably of different periods, peculiar to the salt tracks.

The instance given in *Early British Trackways* of an alignment ending at Droitwich and passing through these two types of names illustrates this. The ley, starting from the Black Mountains, passes through Whitfield House, the mound at Hereford Castle called Hogg's Mount, White House (Tupsley), White Stone (Withington), Westhide Church, Whitwick Manor, and White House at Suckley.

Radiating from Impney Hill, Droitwich, were found leys (one sighted on the Worcestershire Beacon) passing through the many 'wicks' in the district, as Kenswick, Knightwick, Duckwick, Henwick Church, Lower Wick, and Wick Episcopi; also through Whitton and Wittington Churches, the Lower Wych, and the Upper Wych – the last being the well-known pass or cutting through which a main road passes in the centre of the Malverns.

A short typical salt ley comes through Droitwich town, over Whitton Hill (in its suburbs), lies exactly on a long stretch of Rainbow Hill Road in Worcester City, crosses the Severn at the Cathedral Ferry, through Lower Wick, crosses the Teme at old Powick Bridge, and going through a moat (Moat Court) and Burston Cross (at Winds Point) terminates in the Herefordshire Beacon.

Two types of names now divulged, namely, the 'whites' or 'whits', and secondly the 'wicks', 'weeks,' 'wiches' or 'wyches', have been found to align in other districts, to all appearance being on salt tracks.

To take the 'white' group. There are White Houses by the score. White Wells, White Stones, White Rocks, and White Crosses (two each of the last three items in Herefordshire alone). Then White Ways are found in Gloucestershire, Ludlow district, Dorset and Lulworth, the first an important road called the White Way. Most of these places are quite plainly not so called because they have ever been white. Near Cradley is a Whitman's Hill, perhaps most significant of all, for it was the Whitman who carried the white load of salt and gave name to so many places he travelled through.

The Whiteacres (whence the familiar surname Whitaker) were not called from the whiteness of the ground. Whitehouse Hill, Essex (close by is Salcot and Abbott's Wick), Whiteway Hill, and Whitley Ridge bring us in touch with the high places of the sighted track and the leys passing over them. There is a Whiteley place as well as a Saltley.

The 'wick' group of names have been stated (wrongly, it is here claimed) to be derived from the Latin word for village. There is overwhelming evidence of their connexion with salt production and transit. Alles gives Droitwich as being named Saltwic in AD 716 and 888. 'Domesday Book' repeatedly mentions Manors as being possessed of salt pans or pits at Droitwich – always called 'Wich' – and among these is Topsslage (Tupsley), passed through in the first salt track here detailed, and Ullingwic (Ullingswick) which had 'part saline in Wich'.

Wick, Wich, and Wych, are forms of the same name. The salt-producing towns of Cheshire are Nantwich, Middlewich, and Northwich. The other source of salt was from evaporation at the salt marshes, which are plentiful – under that name and as Salterns and 'Wick Marsh' – on low coasts – as off Essex, and on great river estuaries. The several Wick Marshes have no houses on them, nor has Wick Down, inland on high ground. These places never have been villages. Round Worcester, on the way to Droitwich, the 'wick' places (as Henwick, Rushwick, Northwick) are thick on the ground, and it is impossible to note how the 'Wick Farms' cluster round the coast salt places and ignore the connexion. There is a Wick Lane and a Wick Moor in Somerset, a Lee Wick close to the salty Essex coast; and Wicksters Brook and Bridge, Frampton-on-Severn, might well name the salter or white man.

ROBBIE BURNS

'Epigram on the Roads'

between Kilmarnock and Stewarton

I'm now arrived, thanks to the gods!
   Thro' pathways rough and muddy, –
A certain sign that making roads
   Is not this people's study.
And tho' I'm not with scripture crammed,
   I'm sure the bible says
That heedless sinners shall be damned
   Unless they mend their ways.

WILLIAM HAZLITT

'On Going a Journey'

One of the pleasantest things in the world is going a journey; but I like to go by myself. I can enjoy society in a room; but out-of-doors, nature is company enough for me. I am then never less alone than when alone.

> The fields his study, nature was his book.

I cannot see the wit of walking and talking at the same time. When I am in the country I wish to vegetate like the country. I am not for criticizing hedgerows and black cattle. I go out of town in order to forget the town and all that is in it. There are those who for this purpose go to watering-places, and carry the metropolis with them. I like more elbow-room and fewer encumbrances. I like solitude, when I give myself up to it, for the sake of solitude; nor do I ask for

> a friend in my retreat,
> Whom I may whisper solitude is sweet.

The soul of a journey is liberty, perfect liberty, to think, feel, do, just as one pleases. We go a journey chiefly to be free of all impediments and of all inconveniences; to leave our-selves behind much more to get rid of others . . . Instead of a friend in a postchaise or in a Tilbury, to exchange good things with, and vary the same stale topics over again, for once let me have a truce with impertinence. Give me the clear blue sky over my head, and the green turf beneath my feet, a winding road before me, and a three hours' march to dinner – and then to thinking! It is hard if I cannot start some game on these lone heaths. I laugh, I run, I leap, I sing for joy. From the point of yonder rolling cloud I plunge into my past being, and revel there, as the sun-burnt Indian plunges headlong into the wave that wafts him to his native shore. Then long-forgotten things, like 'sunken wrack and sumless treasuries,' burst upon my eager sight, and I begin to feel, think, and be myself again . . .

I grant there is one subject on which it is pleasant to talk on a journey, and that is, what one shall have for supper when we get to our inn at night. The open air improves this sort of conversation or friendly altercation by setting a keener edge on appetite. Every mile of the road heightens the flavour of the viands we expect at the end of it. How fine it is to enter some old town, walled and turreted, just at the approach of nightfall, or to come to some straggling village, with the lights streaming through the surrounding gloom and then, after inquiring for the best entertainment that the place affords, to 'take one's ease at one's inn'! These eventful moments in our lives' history are too precious, too full of solid, heartfelt happiness to be frittered and dribbled away in imperfect sympathy. I would have them all to myself, and drain them to the last drop: they will do to talk of or to write about afterwards. What a delicate speculation it is, after drinking whole goblets of tea, –

The cups that cheer, but not inebriate –

and letting the fumes ascend into the brain, to sit consider-ing what we shall have for supper – eggs and a rasher, a rabbit smothered in onions, or an excellent veal-cutlet! Sancho in such a situation once fixed upon cow-heel; and his choice, though he could not help it, is not to be disparaged. Then, in the intervals of pictured scenery and

Shandean contemplation, to catch the preparation and the stir in the kitchen. *Procul, O procul este profani!* These hours are sacred to silence and to musing, to be treasured up in the memory, and to feed the source of smiling thoughts hereafter. I would not waste them in idle talk; or if I must have the integrity of fancy broken in upon, I would rather it were by a stranger than a friend. A stranger takes his hue and character from the time and place; he is a part of the furniture and costume of an inn. If he is a Quaker, or from the West Riding of Yorkshire, so much the better. I do not even try to sympathize with him, and he breaks no squares. I associate nothing with my travelling companion but present objects and passing events. In his ignorance of me and my affairs, I in a manner forget myself. But a friend reminds one of other things, rips up old grievances, and destroys the abstraction of the scene. He comes in ungraciously between us and our imaginary character. Something is dropped in the course of conversation that gives a hint of your profession and pursuits; or from having some one with you that knows the less sublime portions of your history, it seems that other people do. You are no longer a citizen of the world; but your 'unhoused free condition is put into circumspection and confine'. The incognito of an inn is one of its striking privileges – 'lord of one's self, uncumbered with a name'. Oh! it is great to shake off the trammels of the world and of public opinion – to lose our importunate, tormenting, everlasting personal identity in the elements of nature, and become the creature of the moment, clear of all ties – to hold to the universe only by a dish of sweetbreads, and to owe nothing but the score of the evening – and no longer seeking for applause and meeting with contempt, to be known by no other title than *the Gentleman in the parlour*!

JOAN DIDION

❦

from *Play It As It Lays*

In the first hot month of the fall after the summer she left Carter (the summer Carter left her, the summer Carter stopped living in the house in Beverly Hills), Maria drove the freeway. She dressed every morning with a greater sense of purpose than she had felt in some time, a cotton skirt, a jersey, sandals she could kick off when she wanted the touch of the accelerator, and she dressed very fast, running a brush through her hair once or twice and tying it back with a ribbon, for it was essential (to pause was to throw herself into unspeakable peril) that she be on the freeway by ten o'clock. Not somewhere on Hollywood Boulevard, not on her way to the freeway, but actually on the freeway. If she was not she lost the day's rhythm, its precariously imposed momentum. Once she was on the freeway and had manoeuvred her way to a fast lane she turned on the radio at high volume and she drove. She drove the San Diego to the Harbour, the Harbour up to the Hollywood, the Hollywood to the Golden State, the Santa Monica, the Santa Ana, the Pasadena, the Ventura. She drove it as a riverman runs a river, every day more attuned to its currents, its deceptions, and just as a riverman feels the pull of the rapids in the lull between sleeping and waking, so Maria lay at night in the still of Beverly Hills and saw the great signs soar overhead at seventy miles an hour, *Normandie ¼ Vermont ¾ Harbour Fwy 1*. Again and again she returned to an intricate stretch just south of the interchange where successful passage from the Hollywood on to the Harbour required a diagonal move across four lanes of traffic. On the afternoon she finally did it without once braking or once losing the beat on the radio she was exhilarated, and that night slept dreamlessly . . . Sleep was essential if she was to be on the freeway by ten o'clock. Sometimes the freeway ran out, in a scrap metal yard in San Pedro or on the main street of Palmdale or out somewhere no place at all where the flawless burning concrete just stopped, turned into common road, abandoned construction sheds rusting beside it. When that happened she would keep in careful control, portage skilfully back, feel for the first time the heavy weight of the becalmed car beneath her and try to keep her eyes on the mainstream, the great pilings, the Cyclone fencing, the deadly oleander, the luminous signs, the organism which absorbed all her reflexes, all her attention.

So that she would not have to stop for food she kept a hard-boiled egg on the passenger seat of the Corvette. She could shell and eat a hard-boiled egg at seventy miles an hour (crack it on the steering wheel, never mind salt, salt bloats, no matter what happened she remembered her body) and she drank Coca-Cola in Union 76 stations, Standard stations, Flying A's. She would stand on the hot pavement and drink the Coke from the bottle and put the bottle back in the rack (she tried always to let the attendant notice her putting the bottle in the rack, a show of thoughtful responsibility, no sardine cans in her sink) and then she would walk to the edge of the concrete and stand, letting the sun dry her damp back. To hear her own voice she would sometimes talk to the attendant, ask advice on oil filters, how much air the tyres should carry, the most efficient route to Foothill Boulevard in West Covina. Then she would retie the ribbon in her hair and rinse her dark glasses in the drinking fountain and be ready to drive again. In the first hot month of the fall after the summer she left

Carter, the summer Carter left her, the summer Carter stopped living in the house in Beverly Hills, a bad season in the city, Maria put seven thousand miles on the Corvette.

THOM GUNN

from 'On the Move'

On motorcycles, up the road, they come:
Small, black, as flies hanging in heat, the Boys,
Until the distance throws them forth, their hum
Bulges to thunder held by calf and thigh.
In goggles, donned impersonality,
In gleaming jackets trophied with the dust,
They strap in doubt – by hiding it, robust –
And almost hear a meaning in their noise.

Exact conclusion of their hardiness
Has no shape yet, but from known whereabouts
They ride, direction where the tyres press.
They scare a flight of birds across the field:
Much that is natural, to the will must yield.
Men manufacture both machine and soul,
And use what they imperfectly control
To dare a future from the taken routes.

It is a part solution, after all.
One is not necessarily discord
On earth; or damned because, half animal,
One lacks direct instinct, because one wakes
Afloat on movement that divides and breaks.
One joins the movement in a valueless world,
Choosing it, till, both hurler and the hurled,
One moves as well, always toward, toward.

A minute holds them, who have come to go:
The self-defined, astride the created will
They burst away; the towns they travel through
Are home for neither bird nor holiness,
For birds and saints complete their purposes.
At worst, one is in motion; and at best,
Reaching no absolute, in which to rest,
One is always nearer by not keeping still.

CHRISTOPHER MARLOWE

from *Tamburlaine*

From Scythia to the oriental plage
Of India, where raging Lantchidol
Beats on the region with his boisterous blows
That never seaman yet discovered . . .

I began to march towards Persia,
Along Armenia and the Caspian Sea,
And thence unto Bythinia . . .

The Euxene Sea north to Natolia,
The Terrene west, the Caspian north-north-east
And on the south Senus Arabicus . . .

I crossed the sea and came to Oblia,
And Nigra Silva, where the devils dance . . .

From thence to Nubia near Borno Lake,
And so along the Ethiopian Sea,
Cutting the tropic line of Capricorn,
I conquered all as far as Zanzibar . . .

I came at last to Graecia, and from thence
To Asia, where I stay against my will,
Which is from Scythia where I first began,
Backward and forwards near five thousand leagues.

JOHN MASEFIELD

from 'Reynard the Fox'

Past Tott Hill Down all snaked with meuses,
Past Clench St Michael and Naunton Crucis,
Over short sweet grass and worn flint arrows
And the three dumb hows of Tencombe Barrows.
By Tencombe Regis and Slaughter's Court
Through the great grass square of Roman Fort;
By Nun's Wood Yews, and the Hungary Hill.
And the Corpse Way Stones all standing still?

EDITH WARTON

Driving with Henry James

Henry James, who was a frequent companion on our English motor-trips, was firmly convinced that, because he lived in England and our chauffeur (an American) did not, it was necessary that the latter should be guided by him through the intricacies of the English countryside. Sign-posts were rare in England in those days, and for many years afterwards . . .

It chanced however that Charles Cook, our faithful and skilful driver, was a born path-finder, while James's sense of direction was non-existent, or rather actively but always erroneously alert; and the consequences of his intervention were always bewildering and sometimes extremely fatigu-ing. The first time that my husband and I went to Lamb House by motor (coming from France) James, who had travelled to Folkestone by train to meet us, insisted on seating himself next to Cook on the plea that the roads across Romney Marsh formed such a tangle that only an old inhabitant could guide us to Rye. The suggestion resulted in our turning around and around in our tracks till long after dark, though Rye, conspicuous on its conical hill, was just ahead of us and Cook could easily have landed us there in time for tea . . .

The most absurd of these episodes occurred on another rainy evening when James and I chanced to arrive at Windsor long after dark. We must have been driven by a strange chauffeur – perhaps Cook was on holiday; at any rate, having fallen into the lazy habit of trusting him to know the way, I found myself at a loss to direct his substitute to the King's Road. While I was hesitating and peering out into the darkness James spied an ancient doddering man who had stopped in the rain to gaze at us. 'Wait a moment, my dear – I'll ask him where we are'; and leaning out he signalled to the spectator.

'My good man, if you'll be good enough to come here, please; a little nearer – so,' and as the old man came up: 'My friend, to put it to you in two words, this lady and I have just arrived here from *Slough*; that is to say, to be more strictly accurate, we have recently *passed through* Slough on our way here, having actually motored to Windsor from Rye, which was our point of departure; and the darkness having overtaken us, we should be much obliged if you would tell us where we now are in relation, say, to the High Street, which, as you of course know, leads to the Castle, after leaving on the left hand the turn down to the railway station.'

I was not surprised to have this extraordinary appeal met by silence, and a dazed expression on the old wrinkled face at the window; nor to have James go on: 'In short, my good man, what I want to put to you in a word is this: supposing we have already (as I have reason to think we have) driven past the turn down to the railway station (which in that case, by the way, would probably not have been on our left hand, but on our right) where are we now in relation to . . .'

'Oh, please,' I interrupted, feeling myself utterly unable to sit through another parenthesis, 'do ask him where the King's Road is.'

'Ah – ? The King's Road? Just so! Quite right! Can you, as a matter of fact, my good man, tell us where, in relation to our present position, the King's Road exactly *is?*'

'Ye're in it,' said the aged face at the window.

JAMES JOYCE

from *Ulysses*

Mr Bloom, strolling towards Brunswick street, smiled. My
missus has just got an. Reedy freckled soprano. Cheesepar-
ing nose. Nice enough in its way: for a little ballad. No guts
in it. You and me, don't you know? In the same boat.
Softsoaping. Give you the needle that would. Can't he hear
the difference? Think he's that way inclined a bit. Against
my grain somehow. Thought that Belfast would fetch him.
I hope that smallpox up there doesn't get worse. Suppose
she wouldn't let herself be vaccinated again. Your wife and
my wife.

Wonder is he pimping after me?

Mr Bloom stood at the corner, his eyes wandering over
the multicoloured hoardings. Cantrell and Cochrane's
Ginger Ale (Aromatic). Clery's summer sale. No, he's going
on straight. Hello. *Leah* tonight: Mrs Bandman Palmer.
Like to see her in that again. *Hamlet* she played last night.
Male impersonator. Perhaps he was a woman. Why
Ophelia committed suicide? Poor papa! How he used to
talk about Kate Bateman in that! Outside the Adelphi in
London waited all the afternoon to get in. Year before I
was born that was: sixty-five. And Ristori in Vienna. What
is this the right name is? By Mosenthal it is. Rachel, is it?
No. The scene he was always talking about where the old
blind Abraham recognizes the voice and puts his fingers
on his face.

– Nathan's voice! His son's voice! I hear the voice of Nathan who left his father to die of grief and misery in my arms, who left the house of his father and left the God of his father.

Every word is so deep, Leopold.

Poor papa! Poor man! I'm glad. I didn't go into the room to look at his face. That day! O dear! O dear! Ffoo! Well, perhaps it was the best for him.

Mr Bloom went round the corner and passed the drooping nags of the hazard. No use thinking of it any more. Nosebag time. Wish I hadn't met that M'Coy fellow.

He came nearer and heard a crunching of gilded oats, the gently champing teeth. Their full buck eyes regarded him as he went by, amid the sweet oaten reek of horsepiss. Their Eldorado. Poor jugginses! Damn all they know or care about anything with their long noses stuck in nosebags. Too full for words. Still they get their feed all right and their doss. Gelded too: a stump of black guttapercha wagging limp between their haunches. Might be happy all the same that way. Good poor brutes they look. Still their neigh can be very irritating.

He drew the letter from his pocket and folded it into the newspaper he carried. Might just walk into her here. The lane is safer.

He passed the cabman's shelter. Curious the life of drifting cabbies, all weathers, all places, time or setdown, no will of their own. *Voglio e non.* Like to give them an odd cigarette. Sociable. Shout a few flying syllables as they pass. He hummed:

> *Là ci darem la mano*
> *La la lala la la.*

He turned into Cumberland street and, going on some paces, halted in the lee of the station wall. No one. Meade's timberyard. Piled balks. Ruins and tenements. With careful tread he passed over a hopscotch court with its forgotten pickeystone. Not a sinner. Near the timberyard a squatted child at marbles, alone, shooting the taw with a cunnythumb. A wise tabby, a blinking sphinx, watched from her warm sill. Pity to disturb them. Mohammed cut a piece out of his mantle not to wake her. Open it. And once I played marbles when I went to that old dame's school. She liked mignonette. Mrs Ellis's. And Mr? He opened the letter within the newspaper.

A flower. I think it's a. A yellow flower with flattened petals. Not annoyed then? What does she say?

Dear Henry,

I got your last letter to me and thank you very much for it. I am sorry you did not like my last letter. Why did you enclose the stamps? I am awfully angry with you. I do wish I could punish you for that. I called you naughty boy because I do not like that other word. Please tell me what is the real meaning of that word. Are you not happy in your home you poor little naughty boy? I do wish I could do something for you. Please tell me what you think of poor me. I often think of the beautiful name you have. Dear Henry, when will we meet? I think of you so often you have no idea. I have never felt myself so much drawn to a man as you. I feel so bad about. Please write me a long letter and tell me more. Remember if you do not I will punish you. So now you know what I will do to you, you naughty boy, if you do not write. O how I long to meet you. Henry dear, do not deny my request before my patience are exhausted. Then I will tell you all. Goodbye now, naughty darling. I have such a bad headache today and write *by return* to your longing
                                                                    MARTHA.

P.S. Do tell me what kind of perfume does your wife use. I want to know.

He tore the flower gravely from its pinhold smelt its almost no smell and placed it in his heart pocket. Language of flowers. They like it because no one can hear. Or a poison bouquet to strike him down. Then, walking slowly forward, he read the letter again, murmuring here and there a word. Angry tulips with you darling manflower punish your cactus if you don't please poor forgetmenot how I long violets to dear roses when we soon anemone meet all naughty nightstalk wife Martha's perfume. Having read it all he took it from the newspaper and put it back in his sidepocket.

Weak joy opened his lips. Changed since the first letter. Wonder did she write it herself. Doing the indignant: a girl of good family like me, respectable character. Could meet one Sunday after the rosary. Thank you: not having any. Usual love scrimmage. Then running round corners. Bad as a row with Molly. Cigar has a cooling effect. Narcotic. Go further next time. Naughty boy: punish: afraid of words, of course. Brutal, why not? Try it anyhow. A bit at a time.

Fingering still the letter in his pocket he drew the pin out of it. Common pin, eh? He threw it on the road. Out of her clothes somewhere: pinned together. Queer the number of pins they always have. No roses without thorns.

Flat Dublin voices bawled in his head.

'On Raglan Road'

On Raglan Road on an autumn day I met her first and knew
That her dark hair would weave a snare that I might one
    day rue;
I saw the danger, yet I walked along the enchanted way,
And I said, let grief be a fallen leaf at the dawning of the day.

On Grafton Street in November we tripped lightly along the
    ledge
Of the deep ravine where can be seen the worth of passion's
    pledge,
The Queen of Hearts still making tarts and I not making
    hay –
O I loved too much and by such by such is happiness
    thrown away.

I gave her gifts of the mind I gave her the secret sign that's
    known
To the artists who have known the true gods of sound and
    stone
And word and tint. I did not stint for I gave her poems to
    say.
With her own name there and her own dark hair like clouds
    over fields of May.

On a quiet street where old ghosts meet I see her walking
   now
Away from me so hurriedly my reason must allow
That I wooed not as I should a creature made of clay –
When the angel wooes the clay he'd lose his wings at the
   dawn of day.

FRANK O'HARA

'The Day Lady Died'

It is 12:20 in New York a Friday
three days after Bastille day, yes
it is 1959 and I go get a shoeshine
because I will get off the 4:19 in Easthampton
at 7:15 and then go straight to dinner
and I don't know the people who will feed me

I walk up the muggy street beginning to sun
and have a hamburger and a malted and buy
an ugly NEW WORLD WRITING to see what the poets
in Ghana are doing these days
                            I go on to the bank
and Miss Stillwagon (first name Linda I once heard)
doesn't even look up my balance for once in her life
and in the GOLDEN GRIFFIN I get a little Verlaine
for Patsy with drawings by Bonnard although I do
think of Hesiod, trans. Richmond Lattimore or
Brendan Behan's new play or *Le Balcon* or *Les Nègres*
of Genet, but I don't, I stick with Verlaine
after practically going to sleep with quandariness

and for Mike I just stroll into the PARK LANE
Liquor Store and ask for a bottle of Strega and
then I go back where I came from to 6th Avenue
and the tobacconist in the Ziegfeld Theatre and

casually ask for a carton of Gauloises and a carton
of Picayunes, and a NEW YORK POST with her face on it

and I am sweating a lot by now and thinking of
leaning on the john door in the 5 SPOT
while she whispered a song along the keyboard
to Mal Waldron and everyone and I stopped breathing

THOMAS CORYATE

♥

Title-page of *Crudities*

CORYATS
CRUDITIES

Hastily gobbled up in five
Moneths travells in France
Savoy, Italy, Rhetia commonly
called the Grisons country, Hel
vetia alias Switzerland, some
parts of High Germany, and the
Netherlands;
Newly digested in the hungry aire
of ODCOMBE in the County of
Somerset, & now dispersed to the
nourishment of the travelling mem
[bers of this Kingdome.]

Quadrigis, pedibus bene vivere, navibus atq

GUILLAUME APOLLINAIRE

from *Zone*

Now you walk in Paris alone among the crowd
Herds of bellowing buses hemming you about
Anguish of love parching you within
As though you were never to be loved again
If you lived in olden times you would get you to a cloister
You are ashamed when you catch yourself at a
    paternoster
You are your own mocker and like hellfire your laughter
    crackles
Golden on your life's hearth fall the sparks of your
    laughter
It is a picture in a dark museum hung
And you sometimes go and contemplate it long

Today you walk in Paris the women are blood-red
It was and would I could forget it was at beauty's ebb

From the midst of fervent flames Our Lady beheld me at
    Chartres
The blood of your Sacred Heart flooded me in
    Montmartre
I am sick with hearing the words of bliss
The love I endure is like a syphilis

And the image that possesses you and never leaves your
    side
In anguish and insomnia keeps you alive

Now you are on the Riviera among
The lemon-trees that flower all year long
With your friends you go for a sail on the sea
One is from Nice one from Menton and two from La Turbie
The octopuses in the depths fill us with horror
And in the seaweed fishes swim emblems of the Saviour

You are in an inn-garden near Prague
You feel perfectly happy a rose is on the table
And you observe instead of writing your story in prose
The chafer asleep in the heart of the rose

Appalled you see your image in the agates of Saint Vitus
That day you were fit to die with sadness
You look like Lazarus frantic in the daylight
The hands of the clock in the Jewish quarter go to left from
    right
And you too live slowly backwards
Climbing up to the Hradchin or listening as night falls
To Czech songs being sung in taverns

Here you are in Marseilles among the water-melons

Here you are in Coblenz at the Giant's Hostelry

Here you are in Rome under a Japanese medlar-tree

Here you are in Amsterdam with an ill-favoured maiden
You find her beautiful she is engaged to a student in Leyden
There they let their rooms in Latin cubicula locanda
I remember I spent three days there and as many in Gouda
You are in Paris with the examining magistrate
They clap you in gaol like a common reprobate

74

Grievous and joyous voyages you made
Before you knew what falsehood was and age
At twenty you suffered from love and at thirty again
My life was folly and my days in vain
You dare not look at your hands tears haunt my eyes
For you for her I love and all the old miseries

Provisions List for Sir Francis Drake's West Indian Voyage (1585)

The proporecon of vyctuall for a 100 men

Beef and Porke in hogsheds	12
New land Fyshe	30C
Pylchers in hogsheds	30
Lyngs Cod in Burthens	10 burthens
Bysket in hundreths	10,000 wayght
Meale in Barrclls	22½
Otmeale in barrells	2
Pese in hogsheds	15
Canari wyne in pypes	6
French wyne	1 tone
Bere	30 tonnes

Besydes bacon, butter, chese, honeye, oyle, vynegar, Rye, whereof there is provyded a good quantyty, but the partycular proporcens for each Shyp ys not yet set down at the tyme of the wrytynge here of.

RICHARD HAKLUYT

For banketting on shipboord persons of credit

First the sweetest perfumes to set under hatches to make ye place sweet against theyr comming aboord, if you arrive at Cambalu, Quinsey, or in any such great citie & not among Savages.

Marmelade.	} {	Figs barrelled.
Sucket.		Reisins of the sunne.

Comfets of divers kindes, made of purpose by him that is most excellent, that shall not dissolve.

Prunes damaske.	} {	Walnuts.
Dryed peares.		Almonds. Smalnuts.

Olives to make them taste theyr wine.

The apple John that dureth two yeeres to make shew of our fruits.

Hullocke.	} {	Sacke.

Vials of good sweet waters, and casting bottles of glasses to besprinkle the gests withall, after theyr comming aboord.

Suger, to use with theyr wine, if they will.

The sweet oyle of Santie, and excellent French vineger, and a fine kind of Bisket stiped in the same doe make a banketting dish, and a little Suger cast in it cooleth and comforteth, and refresheth the spirits of man.

Cynomom water	is to be had with you to make a shew of by taste, and also to comfort your sicke in the voyage.
Imperiall Water	

With these and such like, you may banket where you arrive the greater and best persons.

Or with the gift of these Marmelades in small boxes, or small viols of sweet waters you may gratifie by way of gift, or you may make a merchandize of them.

DANIEL DEFOE

❧

from *The Life and Adventures of Robinson Crusoe*

The sea, having hurried me along as before, landed me, or
rather dashed me, against a piece of a rock, and that with
such force as it left me senseless, and indeed helpless, as to
my own deliverance; for the blow taking my side and
breast, beat the breath, as it were, quite out of my body,
and, had it returned again immediately, I must have been
strangled in the water; but I recovered a little before the
return of the waves, and, seeing I should be covered again
with the water, I resolved to hold fast by a piece of the rock,
and so to hold my breath, if possible, till the wave went
back. Now, as the waves were not so high as at first, being
near land, I held my hold till the wave abated, and then
fetched another run, which brought me so near the shore,
that the next wave, though it went over me, yet did not so
swallow me up as to carry me away; and the next run I took
I got to the mainland, where, to my great comfort, I
clambered up the clifts of the shore, and sat me down upon
the grass, free from danger, and quite out of the reach of the
water.

I was now landed, and safe on shore, and began to look
up and thank God that my life was saved, in a case wherein
there was, some minutes before, scarce any room to hope.
I believe it is impossible to express to the life what the
ecstasies and transports of the soul are when it is so saved,

as I may say, out of the very grave; and I do not wonder, now, at that custom, namely, that when a malefactor, who has the halter about his neck, is tied up, and just going to be turned off, and has a reprieve brought to him – I say, I do not wonder that they bring a surgeon with it, to let him blood that very moment they tell him of it, that the surprise may not drive the animal spirits from the heart, and overwhelm him:

For sudden joys, like griefs, confound at first.

I walked about on the shore, lifting up my hands, and my whole being, as I may say, wrapt up in the contemplation of my deliverance, making a thousand gestures and motions which I cannot describe – reflecting upon all my comrades that were drowned, and that there should not be one soul saved but myself – for, as for them, I never saw them afterwards, or any sign of them, except three of their hats, one cap, and two shoes that were not fellows.

I cast my eyes to the stranded vessel, when, the breach and froth of the sea being so big, I could hardly see it, it lay so far off, and considered, Lord! how was it possible I could get on shore?

After I had solaced my mind with the comfortable part of my condition, I began to look round me, to see what kind of place I was in, and what was next to be done; and I soon found my comforts abate, and that in a word, I had a dreadful deliverance: for I was wet, had no clothes to shift me, nor any thing either to eat or drink to comfort me; neither did I see any prospect before me but that of perishing with hunger, or being devoured by wild beasts; and that which was particularly afflicting to me was, that I had no weapon either to hunt and kill any creature for my sustenance, or to defend myself against any other creature that might desire to kill me for theirs – in a word, I had nothing about me but a knife, a tobacco-pipe, and a little tobacco in a box; this was all my provision, and this threw me into terrible agonies of mind, that, for a while, I ran about like a madman. Night coming upon me, I began, with a heavy heart, to consider what would be my lot if there were any ravenous beasts in that country, seeing at night they always come abroad for their prey.

All the remedy that offered to my thoughts at that time was, to get up into a thick bushy tree like a fir, but thorny, which grew near me, and where I resolved to sit all night, and consider the next day what death I should die, for as yet I saw no prospect of life. I walked about a furlong from the shore to see if I could find any fresh water to drink, which I did, to my great joy; and having drunk, and put a little tobacco in my mouth to prevent hunger, I went to the tree, and getting up into it, endeavoured to place myself so as that if I should sleep I might not fall; and having cut me a short stick, like a truncheon, for my defence, I took up my lodging; and, having been excessively fatigued, I fell fast asleep, and slept as comfortably as, I believe, few could have done in my condition, and found myself the most refreshed with it that I think I ever was on such an occasion . . .

My next work was to view the country, and seek a proper place for my habitation, and where to stow my goods, to secure them from whatever might happen. Where I was I yet knew not; whether on the continent or on an island – whether inhabited or not inhabited – whether in danger of wild beasts or not. There was a hill not above a mile from me, which rose up very steep and high, and which seemed to overtop some other hills which lay as in a ridge from it northward. I took out one of the fowling-pieces, and one of the pistols, and a horn of powder; and thus armed, I travelled for discovery up to the top of that hill, where, after I had with great labour and difficulty got to the top, I saw my fate to my great affliction, namely, that I was in an island, environed every way with the sea – no land to be seen, except some rocks which lay a great way off, and two small islands less than this, which lay about three leagues to the west.

I found also, that the island I was in was barren, and, as I saw good reason to believe, uninhabited, except by wild beasts, of which, however, I saw none; yet I saw abundance of fowls, but knew not their kinds; neither, when I killed them, could I tell what was fit for food, and what not. At my coming back, I shot at a great bird, which I saw sitting upon a tree on the side of a great wood; I believe it was the first gun that had been fired there since the creation of the world. I had no sooner fired, but, from all parts of the wood, there arose an innumerable number of fowls of many sorts, making a confused screaming, and crying every one according to his usual note; but not one of them of any kind that I knew. As for the creature I killed, I took it to be a kind of hawk, its colour and beak resembling it, but had no talons, or claws, more than common; its flesh was carrion, and fit for nothing.

Contented with this discovery, I came back to my raft, and fell to work to bring my cargo on shore, which took me up the rest of that day.

WOODES ROGERS

❧

The Rescue of Alexander Selkirk,*
Juan Fernández Islands, Chile
(2 February 1709)

Our pinnace return'd from the shore, and brought a man
cloth'd in goatskins, who look'd wilder than the first
owners of them. He had been on the island four years and
four months, being left there by Captain Stradling in the
Cinque-Ports. His name was Alexander Selkirk, a Scotch-
man, who had been Master of the *Cinque-Ports*, a ship that
came here last with Captain Dampier . . . He told us he was
born at Largo in the county of Fife, Scotland, and was bred a
sailor from his youth. The reason of his being left here was a
difference betwixt him and his captain . . . He had with him
his clothes and bedding, with a firelock, some powder,
bullets, and tobacco, a hatchet, a knife, a kettle, a Bible,
some practical pieces, and his mathematical instruments
and books.

He diverted and provided for himself as well as he could;
but for the first eight months had much ado to bear up
against melancholy, and the terror of being left alone in
such a desolate place. He built two huts with piemento trees,
cover'd them with long grass, and lin'd them with the skins
of goats which he killed with his gun as he wanted, so long

* The model for Robinson Crusoe.

as his powder lasted, which was but a pound, and that being near spent, he got fire by rubbing two sticks of piemento wood together upon his knee. In the lesser hut, at some distance from the other, he dressed his victuals, and in the larger he slept, and employed himself in reading, singing Psalms, and praying, so that he said he was a better Christian while in this solitude, than ever he was before, or than he was afraid he should ever be again. At first he never eat anything till hunger constrain'd him, partly for grief, and partly for want of bread and salt; nor did he go to bed till he could watch no longer. The piemento wood, which burnt very clear, serv'd him both for firing and candle, and refresh'd him with its fragrant smell. He might have had fish enough, but could not eat 'em for want of salt, because they occasion'd a looseness; except Crawfish, which are there as large as lobsters and very good. These he sometimes boiled, and at other times broiled as he did his goats' flesh, of which he made very good broth, for they are not so rank as ours; he kept an account of 500 that he kill'd while there, and caught as many more, which he marked on the ear and let go. When his powder fail'd he took them by speed of foot; for his way of living, and continual exercise of walking and running, clear'd him of all gross humours, so that he ran with wonderful swiftness thro the woods, and up the rocks and hills, as we perceiv'd when we employ'd him to catch goats for us. We had a bull dog which we sent with several of our nimblest runners to help him in catching goats; but he distanc'd and tir'd both the dog and the men, catch'd the goats and brought 'em to us on his back . . . He soon wore out all his shoes and clothes by running thro the woods; and at last, being forced to shift without them, his feet became so hard that he ran everywhere without annoyance, and it was some time before he could wear shoes after we found him. For not being used to any so long, his feet swelled when he came first to wear 'em again. After he had conquer'd his melancholy he diverted himself sometimes by cutting his name on the trees, and the time of his being left and continuance there. He was at first much pester'd with cats and rats, that had bred in great numbers from some of each species which had got ashore from ships that put in there to wood and water. The rats gnaw'd his feet and clothes while asleep, which obliged him to cherish the cats with his goats' flesh; by which many of them became so tame that they would lie about him in hundreds, and soon deliver'd him from the rats.

He likewise tam'd some kids, and to divert himself would now and then sing and dance with them and his cats; so that by the care of Providence, and vigour of his youth, being now about 30 years old, he came at last to conquer all the inconveniences of his solitude and to be very easy. When his clothes wore out he made himself a coat and cap of goatskins, which he stitch'd together with little thongs of the same that he cut with his knife. He had no other needle but a nail, and when his knife was wore to the back, he made others as well as he could of some iron hoops that were left ashore, which he beat thin and ground upon stones. Having some linen cloth by him, he sow'd himself shirts with a nail and stitch'd 'em with the worsted of his old stockings, which he pull'd out on purpose. He had his last shirt on when we found him in the island.

At his first coming on board us, he had so much forgot his language for want of use, that we could scarce understand him, for he seemed to speak his words by halves. We offer'd him a dram, but he would not touch it, having drank nothing but water since his being there, and 'twas some time before he could relish our victuals.

ALEXANDER SELKIRK

I shall never be so happy as when I was not worth a farthing.

HAROLD BRIDE

The *Titanic*: The Wireless Operator's Story, 15 April 1912

From aft came the tunes of the band. It was a ragtime tune. I don't know what. Then there was 'Autumn' . . . I went to the place I had seen the collapsible boat on the boat deck, and to my surprise I saw the boat, and the men still trying to push it off. I guess there wasn't a sailor in the crowd. They couldn't do it. I went up to them and was just lending a hand when a large wave came awash of the deck. The big wave carried the boat off. I had hold of an oarlock and I went with it. The next I knew I was in the boat. But that was not all. I was in the boat, and the boat was upside-down, and I was under it. And I remember realizing I was wet through and that whatever happened I must not breathe, for I was under water. I knew I had to fight for it, and I did. How I got out from under the boat I do not know but I felt a breath of air at last. There were men all around me – hundreds of them. The sea was dotted with them, all depending on their lifebelts. I felt I simply had to get away from the ship. She was a beautiful sight then. Smoke and sparks were rushing out of her funnel. There must have been an explosion, but we heard none. We only saw the big stream of sparks. The ship was turning gradually on her nose – just like a duck that goes for a dive. I had only one thing on my mind – to get away from the suction. The band was still playing. I guess all of them went down. They were playing 'Autumn' then. I swam with all my might. I suppose I was 150 feet away when the *Titanic*, on her nose, with her after-quarter sticking straight up in the air, began to settle – slowly.

When at last the waves washed over her rudder there wasn't the least bit of suction I could feel. She must have kept going just so slowly as she had been . . . I felt after a little while like sinking. I was very cold. I saw a boat of some kind near me, and put all my strength into an effort to swim to it. It was hard work. I was all done when a hand reached out from the boat and pulled me aboard. It was our same collapsible. The same crowd was on it. There was just room for me to roll on the edge. I lay there not caring what happened. Somebody sat on my legs. They were wedged in between slats and were being wrenched. I had not the heart left to ask the man to move. It was a terrible sight all around – men swimming and sinking.

I lay where I was, letting the man wrench my feet out of shape. Others came near. Nobody gave them a hand. The bottom-up boat already had more men than it would hold, and it was sinking. At first the larger waves splashed over my clothing. Then they began to splash over my head, and I had to breathe when I could. As we floated around on our capsized boat and I kept straining my eyes for a ship's lights, somebody said, 'Don't the rest of you think we ought to pray?' The man who made the suggestion asked what the religion of the others was. Each man called out his religion. One was a Catholic, one a Methodist, one a Presbyterian. It was decided the most appropriate prayer for all was the Lord's Prayer.

HESKETH PEARSON

❧

Oscar Wilde's Arrival at New York, 1882

The reporters who mobbed him on the boat were a little downcast by his appearance, which was more like that of an athlete than an aesthete. True, he had long hair, and he wore a bottle-green fur-lined overcoat, with a round seal-skin cap on his head, but he was a giant in stature and his fists looked formidable. He naturally expected them to question him concerning his mission; instead they asked him how he liked his eggs fried, what he slept in, how he trimmed his finger-nails, and what temperature he liked his bath to be. His answers displayed a lack of interest in the questions, and they button-holed the passengers for something of a livelier nature. The passengers rose to the occasion: they had heard him complain that the trip was tame, 'deucedly stupid' in fact, that the roaring ocean did not roar, and that nothing less than a storm which swept the bridge from the ship would give him any pleasure. That was enough for the reporters, who told their readers that Wilde was 'disappointed with the Atlantic Ocean', a phrase which got him far more publicity than his views on aestheticism would have done, or even a sparkling riposte on the theme of fried eggs. Wilde realized that he had not done himself justice on the boat, so made up for it the moment he stepped ashore. 'Have you anything to declare?' asked the customs official. 'No. I have nothing to declare'; he paused: 'except my genius.' Few remarks in history have travelled as widely and quickly as that one.

WILLIAM WORDSWORTH

from *The Prelude*

One evening (surely I was led by her)
I went alone into a Shepherd's Boat
A Skiff that to a Willow tree was tied
Within a rocky Cave, its usual home.
'Twas by the shores of Patterdale, a Vale
Wherein I was a Stranger, thither come
A School-boy Traveller, at the Holidays.
Forth rambled from the Village Inn alone
No sooner had I sight of this small Skiff,
Discover'd thus by unexpected chance,
Than I unloosed her tether and embarked.
The moon was up, the Lake was shining clear
Among the hoary mountains; from the Shore
I pushed, and struck the oars and struck again
In cadence, and my little Boat mov'd on
Even like a Man who walks with stately step
Though bent on speed. It was an act of stealth
And troubled pleasure; not without the voice
Of mountain-echoes did my Boat move on,
Leaving behind her still on either side
Small circles glittering idly in the moon,
Until they melted all into one track
Of sparkling light. A rocky Steep uprose
Above the Cavern of the Willow tree
And now, as suited one who proudly row'd

With his best skill, I fix'd a steady view
Upon the top of that same craggy ridge,
The bound of the horizon, for behind
Was nothing but the stars and the grey sky.
She was an elfin Pinnace; lustily
I dipped my oars into the silent Lake,
And, as I rose upon the stroke, my Boat
Went heaving through the water, like a Swan;
When from behind that craggy Steep, till then
The bound of the horizon, a huge Cliff,
As if with voluntary power instinct,
Upreared its head. I struck, and struck again,
And growing still in stature, the huge Cliff
Rose up between me and the stars, and still,
With measur'd motion, like a living thing,
Strode after me. With trembling hands I turned,
And through the silent water stole my way
Back to the Cavern of the Willow tree.
There, in her mooring-place, I left my Bark,
And, through the meadows homeward went, with grave
And serious thoughts; and after I had seen
That spectacle, for many days, my brain
Worked with a dim and undetermin'd sense
Of unknown modes of being; in my thoughts
There was a darkness, call it solitude,
Or blank desertion, no familiar shapes
Of hourly objects, images of trees,
Of sea or sky, no colours of green fields;
But huge and mighty Forms that do not live
Like living men mov'd slowly through the mind
By day and were the trouble of my dreams.

JOSEPH CONRAD

♥

from *Heart of Darkness*

'Going up that river was like travelling back to the earliest beginnings of the world, when vegetation rioted on the earth and the big trees were kings. An empty stream, a great silence, an impenetrable forest. The air was warm, thick, heavy, sluggish. There was no joy in the brilliance of sunshine. The long stretches of the waterway ran on, deserted, into the gloom of overshadowed distances. On silvery sandbanks hippos and alligators sunned themselves side by side. The broadening waters flowed through a mob of wooded islands; you lost your way on that river as you would in a desert, and butted all day long against shoals, trying to find the channel, till you thought yourself be-witched and cut off for ever from everything you had known once – somewhere – far away – in another existence perhaps. There were moments when one's past came back to one, as it will sometimes when you have not a moment to spare to yourself; but it came in the shape of an unrestful and noisy dream, remembered with wonder amongst the overwhelming realities of this strange world of plants, and water, and silence. And this stillness of life did not in the least resemble a peace. It was the stillness of an implacable force brooding over an inscrutable intention. It looked at you with a vengeful aspect . . . The reaches opened before us and closed behind, as if the forest had stepped leisurely across the water to bar the way for our return. We penetrated deeper and deeper into the heart of darkness. It was very quiet there. At night sometimes the roll of drums behind the curtain of trees would run up the river and remain sustained faintly, as if hovering in the air high over our heads, till the first break of day. Whether it meant war, peace, or prayer we could not tell . . . We were wanderers on prehistoric earth, on an earth that wore the aspect of an unknown planet. We could have fancied ourselves the first of men taking possession of an accursed inheritance, to be subdued at the cost of profound anguish and of excessive toil. But suddenly, as we struggled round a bend, there would be a glimpse of rush walls, of peaked grass-roofs, a burst of yells, a whirl of black limbs, a mass of hands clapping, of feet stamping, of bodies swaying, of eyes rolling, under the droop of heavy and motionless foliage. The steamer toiled along slowly on the edge of a black and incomprehensible frenzy. The prehistoric man was cursing us, praying to us, welcoming us – who could tell? We were cut off from the comprehension of our surroundings; we glided past like phantoms, wondering and secretly appalled, as sane men would be before an enthusiastic outbreak in a madhouse. We could not understand because we were too far and could not remember, because we were travelling in the night of first ages, of those ages that are gone, leaving hardly a sign – and no memories.

'The earth seemed unearthly. We are accustomed to look upon the shackled form of a conquered monster, but there – there you could look at a thing monstrous and free. It was unearthly, and the men were – No, they were not inhuman. Well, you know, that was the worst of it – this suspicion of their not being inhuman. It would come slowly to one. They howled and leaped, and spun, and made horrid faces; but what thrilled you was just the thought of their humanity – like yours – the thought of your remote kinship with this wild and passionate uproar. Ugly. Yes, it was ugly enough; but if you were man enough you would admit to yourself that there was in you just the faintest trace of a response to the terrible frankness of that noise, a dim suspicion of there being a meaning in it which you – you so remote from the night of first ages – could comprehend. And why not? The mind of man is capable of anything – because everything is in it, all the past as well as all the future.

SIR WALTER RALEGH

from *The Discoverie of Guiana*

The farther we went on (our victuall decreasing and the aire
breeding great faintnes) we grew weaker and weaker when
we had most need of strength and abilitie, for howerlie the
river ran more violently than other against us, and the
barge, wherries, and ships bote of Captaine *Gifford*, and
Captaine *Calfield*, had spent all their provisions, so as wee
were brought into despaire and discomfort, had we not
perswaded all the companie that it was but onlie one daies
worke more to attaine the lande where we should be
releeved of all we wanted, and if we returned that we were
sure to starve by the way, and that the worlde would also
laugh us to scorne. On the banks of these rivers were divers
sorts of fruits good to eate, flowers and trees of that varietie
as were sufficient to make ten volumes of herbals, we
releeved our selves manie times with the fruits of the
countrey, and somtimes with foule and fish: we sawe birds
of all colours, some carnation, some crimson, orenge
tawny, purple, greene, watched, and of all other sorts both
simple and mixt, as it was unto us a great good passing of
the time to beholde them, besides the reliefe we found by
killing some store of them with our fouling peeces, without
which, having little or no bread and lesse drink, but onely
the thick and troubled water of the river, we had been in a
very hard case.

Our old Pilot of the *Ciawani* (whom, as I said before, we

tooke to redeeme *Ferdinando*,) told us, that if we would enter a branch of a river on the right hand with our barge and wherries, and leave the *Galley* at ancor the while in the great river, he would bring us to a towne of the *Arwacas* where we should find store of bread, hens, fish, and of the countrey wine, and perswaded us that departing from the *Galley* at noone, we might returne ere night: I was very glad to heare this speech, and presently tooke my barge, with eight musketiers, Captain *Giffords* wherrie, with himselfe and foure musketiers, and Captaine *Calfield* with his wherrie and as manie, and so we entred the mouth of this river, and bicause we were perswaded that it was so neere, we tooke no victuall with us at all: when we had rowed three howres, we marvelled we sawe no signe of any dwelling, and asked the Pilot where the town was, he told us a little farther: after three howers more the *Sun* being almost set, we began to suspect that he led us that waie to betraie us, for he confessed that those Spaniards which fled from *Trinedado*, and also those that remained with *Carapana* in *Emeria*, were joyned togither in some village upon that river. But when it grew towardes night, and we demaunding where the place was, he tolde us but fower reaches more; when we had rowed fower and fower, we saw no signe, and our poore water men even hart broken, and tired, were ready to giue up the ghost; for we had now come from the *Galley* neer forty miles.

At the last we determined to hang the Pilot, and if we had well knowen the way backe againe by night, he had surely gone, but our owne necessities pleaded sufficiently for his safetie: for it was as darke as pitch, and the river began so to narrow it selfe, and the trees to hang over from side to side, as we were driven with arming swordes to cut a passage thorow those branches that covered the water. We were very desirous to finde this towne hoping of a feast, bicause we made but a short breakfast aboord the *Galley* in the morning, and it was now eight a clock at night, and our stomacks began to gnaw apace: but whether it was best to returne or go on, we began to doubt, suspecting treason in the Pilot more and more: but the poore old Indian ever assured us that it was but a little farther, and but this one turning, and that turning, and at last about one a clocke after midnight we saw a light, and rowing towards it, we heard the dogs of the village.

ALVAR NUÑEZ CABEZA DE VACA

❧

from *The Marvellous Adventure of Cabeza de Vaca*

This is the tale of what men can and cannot do when they must do something or die.

You will understand what I am not telling you: that I saw men jump overboard, mad from thirst and sun. That I saw them swell and die slowly in delirium, heard their words and songs put out the pitiful contents of their minds. That I saw men gnaw at corpses. And that these were Spanish gentlemen.

It is curious to have so graphic a lesson in what life may become. We had been a proud band, relying on our united strength, our armour and our horses. Slowly our strength disunited, until nothing that we had in common remained to help any of us.

As I say, it is curious when one has nobody and nothing to rely upon outside of oneself.

While we were subjects of Your Majesty we had everything life offers, and now we had nothing. To understand what it means to have nothing one must have nothing. No clothing against the weather might appear the worst. But for us poor skeletons who survived it, it was not.

The worst lay in parting little by little with the thoughts that clothe the soul of a European, and most of all with the idea that a man attains strength through dirk and dagger, and serving Your Majesty's Guard. We had to surrender such fantasies till our inward nakedness was the nakedness of an unborn babe, starting life anew in a womb of sensations which in themselves can mysteriously nourish. Several years went by before I could relax in that living plexus for which even now I have no name; but only when at last I relaxed could I see the possibilities of a life in which to be deprived of Europe was not to be deprived of too much.

Being Europeans, we thought we had given away to doctors and priests our ability to heal. But here it was, still in our possession, even if we had only Indians to exercise it upon. It was ours after all; we were more than we had thought we were.

To be more than I thought I was – a sensation utterly new to me.

Starvation, nakedness, slavery: sensations utterly new to me, also.

PAULETTE JILES

❥

'Night Flight to Attiwapiskat'

We are flying directly into darkness, the
dim polestar rides on the starboard wing, Orion
and his blue gems freeze in the southwest.

Our rare and singular lives are in the hands of the
pilot; after him the radar and one engine. There were
two engines when we started out but the other one
died. We watch

the starboard propeller feather in slow, coarse
revolutions. The pilot says we will make Attiwapiskat or
some place.
                Icarus, our pilot and our downfall.

Two thousand feet below dim lakes pour past as if
on their way to a laundromat. How could we have
sunk so low?
At times like this I consider life after death
as if it were a binary system, there are
no half-lives. We track cautiously down
the Milky Way, home of nebulae and Cygnus.

We are footloose in the corridors of the aurora.

The long stream of my life is flying out behind
this airplane like skywriting on the subarctic
night, fluttering, whipped with urgency. Each
episode was always cut off from the last, I used
to find myself a series of hostile strangers, startled
in doorways. Now they

gather themselves up, the wives, daughters, friends,
victims, perpetrators, the one with the pen and the
other carrying a blank mask, another at present
at the cleaners.

They catch up and slam together like
a deck of cards, packed into the present
moment. Is there a soul in there, a queen?
I draw one out; it's the ace of airplanes.
The radar repeats a fixed,

green idea. The pilot feels for the radio touch
of Thunder Bay.

At a thousand feet we make quick decisions
about our loyalties, the other engine might fail,
the suitcases of our hearts might be opened with
all that contraband, the jewels and screams, we
might have things to declare;
    the observable universe is my native country
    poetry is my mother tongue
    the ideas I have purchased on this side of the
border don't amount to more than a hundred dollars.
What comes after this?

What do you mean, what comes after this?
This is it.
Attiwapiskat approaches, a Cree village
on a cold salt coast, flying patchwork quilts in
several more colours than are found in nature,
shining with blue-white runway lights.

We will sleep in the guesthouse tonight, that
refuge of displaced persons. The pilot will
go down and repair the valve and say nothing happened.
(We flew into darkness at the rim of the world,
where distant lights broke through and something
failed us. Then at the edge when we were stamped
and ready to go through we were turned back.) We
can unload and forget it. But I will remember
and then go back and forget again.
This is Attiwapiskat, everything is as it should be.
We slide down to the airstrip through salt fogs
from Hudson Bay that slip through the night like
airborne bedsheets.
We get off, still life with sleeping bags.
Approaching us is an earthman,
speaking Cree.

ROBERT LOWELL

from 'Skunk Hour'

One dark night,
my Tudor Ford climbed the hill's skull,
I watched for love-cars. Lights turned down,
they lay together, hull to hull,
where the graveyard shelves on the town . . .
My mind's not right.

A car radio bleats,
'Love, O careless Love . . .' I hear
my ill-spirit sob in each blood cell,
as if my hand were at its throat . . .
I myself am hell,
nobody's here –

only skunks, that search
in the moonlight for a bite to eat.
They march on their soles up Main Street:
white stripes, moonstruck eyes' red fire
under the chalk-dry and spar spire
of the Trinitarian Church.

I stand on top
of our back steps and breathe the rich air –
a mother skunk with her column of kittens swills the
garbage pail.

She jabs her wedge-head in a cup
of sour cream, drops her ostrich tail,
and will not scare.

FRANCIS GODWIN

A Seventeeth-Century Moon Landing

My Gansas [wild swans] began to bestir themselves, still directing their course toward the Globe or body of the Moone: And they made their way with that incredible swiftnesse, as I thinke they gained not so little as Fifty Leagues in every hower. In that passage I noted three things very remarkeable: one that the further we went, the lesser the Globe of the Earth appeared unto us; whereas the Moone shewed her selfe more and more monstrously huge.

Againe, the Earth (which ever I held in mine eye) did as it were mask itselfe with a kinde of brightnesse like another Moone; and even as in the Moone we discerned certaine spots or Clouds, as it were, so did I then in the earth. But whereas the forme of those spots in the Moone continue constantly one and the same; these little and little did change every hower. The reason thereof I conceive to be this, that whereas the Earth according to her naturall motion, (for that such a motion she hath, I am now constrained to joyne in opinion with Copernicus), turneth round upon her owne Axe every 24 howers from the West unto the East: I should at the first see in the middle of the body of this new starre a spot like unto a Peare that had a morsell bitten out upon the one side of him; after certaine howers, I should see that spot slide away to the East side. This no doubt was the maine of Africa. Then should I perceive a great shining brightnesse to occupy that roome, during the like time (which was undoubtedly none other then the great Atlantick Ocean). After that succeeded a spot almost of an Ovall form, even just such as we see America to have in our Mapps. Then another vast cleernesse representing the West Ocean; and lastly a medly of spots, like the Countries of the East Indies. So that it seemed unto me no other then a huge Mathematicall Globe, leasurely turned before me, wherein successively, all the Countries of our earthly world within the compasse of 24 howers were represented to my sight. And this was all the meanes I had now to number the dayes, and take reckoning of time . . .

But give me leave now at last to passe on my journey quietly, without interruption for Eleven or Twelve daies, during all which time, I was carried directly toward the Globe or body of the Moone with such a violent whirling as cannot bee expressed. For I cannot imagine that a bullet out of the mouth of a Cannon could make way through the vaporous and muddie aire neere the earth with that celerity, which is most strange, considering that my Gansas moved their wings but even now and then, and sometimes not at all in a Quarter of an hower together; only they held them stretched out, so passing on, as we see that Eagles, and Kites sometimes will doe for a little space, and during the time of those pauses I beleeve they tooke their napps and times of sleeping; for other (as I might easily note) they had none.

Now for my selfe, I was so fast knit unto my Engin, as I durst commit my selfe to slumbring enough to serve my turne, which I tooke with as great ease (although I am loath to speake it, because it may seeme incredible) as if I had beene in the best Bed of downe in all Antwerp.

After Eleven daies passage in this violent flight, I perceived that we began to approach neare unto another Earth, if I may so call it, being the Globe or very body of that starre which we call the Moone.

The first difference that I found betweene it and our earth, was, that it shewed it selfe in his naturall colours: as soon as

I was free from the attraction of the Earth; whereas with us, a thing removed from our eye but a league or two, begins to put on that lurid and deadly colour of blue.

Then, I perceived also, that it was covered for the most part with a huge and mighty Sea, those parts only being drie Land, which shew unto us here somewhat darker then the rest of her body that I mean which the Country people call *el hombre della Luna*, the Man in the Moone. As for that part which shineth so clearly in our eyes; it is even another Ocean, yet besprinckled heere and there with Islands, which for the littlenesse, so farre off we cannot discern. So that same splendor appearing unto us, and giving light unto our night, appeareth to be nothing else but the reflexion of the Sun beames returned unto us out of the water, as out of a glasse: How ill this agreeth with that which our Philosophers teach in the schooles I am not ignorant . . .

When by my reckoning it seemed to be (as indeed it was) Tuesday the Eleventh day of September, (at what time the Moone being two daies old was in the Twentieth degree of Libra), my Gansas staied their course as it was with one consent, and tooke their rest, for certaine howers; after which they tooke their flight, and within lesse then one hower, set me upon the top of a very high hill in that other world, where immediately were presented unto mine eyes many most strange and unwonted sights.

For first, I observed, that although the Globe of the Earth shewed much bigger there then the Moone doth unto us, even to the full trebling of her diameter, yet all manner of things there were of largenesse and quantity, 10, 20, I thinke I may say 30 times more then ours. Their trees were at least three times so high as ours, and more then five times the breadth and thicknesse. So were their herbes, Beasts, and Birds; although to compare them with ours I know not well how, because I found not any thing there, any species either of Beast or Bird that resembled ours any thing at all, except Swallowes, Nightingales, Cuckooes, Woodcockes, Batts, and some kindes of wild Fowle, as also of such Birds as my Gansas, all which, (as now I well perceived,) spend the time of their absence from us, even there in that world; neither do they vary any thing at all either in quantity or quality from those of ours heere, as being none other then the very same.

No sooner was I set downe upon the ground, but I was . . . environed with a kind of people most strange, both for their feature, demeanure, and apparell. Their stature was most divers but for the most part, twice the height of ours: their colour and countenance most pleasing, and their habit such, as I know not how to expresse. For neither did I see any kind of Cloth, Silke, or other stuffe to resemble the matter of that whereof their Clothes were made; neither (which is most strange, of all other) can I devise how to describe the colour of them, being in a manner all clothed alike. It was neither blacke, nor white, yellow, nor redd, greene nor blue, nor any colour composed of these. But if you aske me what it was then; I must tell you, it was a colour never seen in our earthly world, and therefore neither to be described unto us by any, nor to be conceived of one that never saw it. For as it were a hard matter to describe unto a man borne blind the difference betweene blue and Greene, so can I not bethinke my selfe any meane how to decipher unto you this Lunar colour, having no affinitie with any other that ever I beheld with mine eyes. Onely this I can say of it, that it was the most glorious and delightfull that can possibly be imagined; neither in truth was there any one thing, that more delighted me, during my abode in that new world, than the beholding of that most pleasing and resplendent colour.

NEIL ARMSTRONG AND EDWIN 'BUZZ' ALDRIN

🌙

Moon Landing, 21 July 1969

NEIL ARMSTRONG The most dramatic recollections I had were the sights themselves. Of all the spectacular views we had, the most impressive to me was on the way to the Moon, when we flew through its shadow. We were still thousands of miles away, but close enough, so that the Moon almost filled our circular window. It was eclipsing the Sun, from our position, and the corona of the Sun was visible around the limb of the Moon as a gigantic lens-shaped or saucer-shaped light, stretching out to several lunar diameters. It was magnificent, but the Moon was even more so. We were in its shadow, so there was no part of it illuminated by the Sun. It was illuminated only by earthshine. It made the Moon appear blue-grey, and the entire scene looked decidedly three-dimensional.

I was really aware, visually aware, that the moon was in fact a sphere not a disc. It seemed almost as if it were showing us its roundness, its similarity in shape to our Earth, in a sort of welcome. I was sure that it would be a hospitable host. It had been awaiting its first visitors for a long time . . .

The sky is black, you know. It's a very dark sky. But it still seemed more like daylight than darkness as we looked out the window. It's a peculiar thing, but the surface looked very warm and inviting. It was the sort of situation in which you felt like going out there in nothing but a swimming suit to get a little sun. From the cockpit, the surface seemed to be tan. It's hard to account for that, because later when I held this material in my hand, it wasn't tan at all. It was black, grey and so on. It's some kind of lighting effect, but out the window the surface looks much more like light desert sand than black sand . . .

EDWIN 'BUZZ' ALDRIN The blue colour of my boot has completely disappeared now into this – still don't know exactly what colour to describe this other than greyish-cocoa colour. It appears to be covering most of the lighter part of my boot . . . very fine particles . . .

Odour is very subjective, but to me there was a distinct smell to the lunar material – pungent, like gunpowder or spent cap-pistol caps. We carted a fair amount of lunar dust back inside the vehicle with us, either on our suits and boots or on the conveyor system we used to get boxes and equipment back inside. We did notice the odour right away.

T. S. ELIOT

'Journey of the Magi'

'A cold coming we had of it,
Just the worst time of the year
For a journey, and such a long journey:
The ways deep and the weather sharp,
The very dead of winter.'
And the camels galled, sore-footed, refractory,
Lying down in the melting snow.
There were times we regretted
The summer palaces on slopes, the terraces,
And the silken girls bringing sherbet.
Then the camel men cursing and grumbling
And running away, and wanting their liquor and women,
And the night-fires going out, and the lack of shelters,
And the cities hostile and the towns unfriendly
And the villages dirty and charging high prices:
A hard time we had of it.
At the end we preferred to travel all night,
Sleeping in snatches,
With the voices singing in our ears, saying
That this was all folly.

Then at dawn we came down to a temperate valley,
Wet, below the snow line, smelling of vegetation,
With a running stream and a water-mill beating the
    darkness,

And three trees on the low sky.
And an old white horse galloped away in the meadow.
Then we came to a tavern with vine-leaves over the lintel,
Six hands at an open door dicing for pieces of silver,
And feet kicking the empty wine-skins.
But there was no information, so we continued
And arrived at evening, not a moment too soon
Finding the place; it was (you may say) satisfactory.

    All this was a long time ago, I remember,
And I would do it again, but set down
This set down
This: were we led all that way for
Birth or Death? There was a Birth, certainly,
We had evidence and no doubt. I had seen birth and death,
But had thought they were different; this Birth was
Hard and bitter agony for us, like Death, our death.
We returned to our places, these Kingdoms,
But no longer at ease here, in the old dispensation,
With an alien people clutching their gods.
I should be glad of another death.

The Journey to Emmaus

And, behold, two of them went that same day to a village called Ĕmmáŭs, which was from Jerusalem about three-score furlongs.

And they talked together of all these things which had happened.

And it came to pass, that, while they communed together and reasoned, Jesus himself drew near, and went with them.

But their eyes were holden that they should not know him.

And he said unto them, What manner of communications are these that ye have one to another, as ye walk, and are sad?

And the one of them, whose name was Clĕŏpăs, answering said unto him, Art thou only a stranger in Jerusalem, and hast not known the things which are come to pass there in these days?

And he said unto them, What things? And they said unto him, Concerning Jesus of Nazareth, which was a prophet mighty in deed and word before God and all the people:

And how the chief priests and our rulers delivered him to be condemned to death, and have crucified him.

But we trusted that it had been he which should have redeemed Israel: and beside all this, to day is the third day since these things were done.

Yea, and certain women also of our company made us astonished, which were early at the sepulchre;

And when they found not his body, they came, saying, that they had also seen a vision of angels, which said that he was alive.

And certain of them which were with us went to the sepulchre, and found it even so as the women had said: but him they saw not.

Then he said unto them, O fools, and slow of heart to believe all that the prophets have spoken:

Ought not Christ to have suffered these things, and to enter into his glory?

And beginning at Moses and all the prophets, he expounded unto them in all the scriptures the things concerning himself.

And they drew nigh unto the village, whither they went: and he made as though he would have gone further.

But they constrained him, saying, Abide with us: for it is toward evening, and the day is far spent. And he went in to tarry with them.

And it came to pass, as he sat at meat with them, he took bread, and blessed it, and brake, and gave to them.

And their eyes were opened, and they knew him; and he vanished out of their sight.

And they said one to another, Did not our heart burn within us, while he talked with us by the way, and while he opened to us the scriptures?

And they rose up the same hour, and returned to Jerusalem, and found the eleven gathered together, and them that were with them

Saying, The Lord is risen indeed, and hath appeared to Simon.

And they told what things were done in the way, and how he was known of them in breaking of bread.

HERODOTUS

❧

In Egypt

The following is the general character of the region. In the first place, on approaching it by sea, when you are still a day's sail from the land, if you let down a sounding-line you will bring up mud, and find yourself in eleven fathoms' water, which shows that the soil washed down by the streams extend to that distance . . . The coast-line of Egypt would extend a length of three thousand six hundred furlongs. From the coast inland as far as Heliopolis the breadth of Egypt is considerable, the country is flat, without springs, and full of swamps. The length of the route from the sea up to Heliopolis is almost exactly the same as that of the road which runs from the altar of the twelve gods at Athens to the temple of Olympian Zeus at Pisa . . . As one proceeds beyond Heliopolis up the country, Egypt becomes narrow, the Arabian range of hills, which has a direction from north to south, shutting it in upon the one side, and the Libyan range upon the other. The former ridge runs on without a break, and stretches away to the sea called the Erythraean; it contains the quarries whence the stone was cut for the pyramids of Memphis: and this is the point where it ceases its first direction, and bends away in the manner above indicated. In its greatest length from east to west it is, as I have been informed, a distance of two months' journey; towards the extreme east its skirts produce frankincense. Such are the chief features of this range. On the Libyan side, the other ridge whereon the pyramids stand, is rocky and covered with sand; its direction is the same as that of the Arabian ridge in the first part of its course. Above Heliopolis, then, there is no great breadth of territory for such a country as Egypt, but during four days' sail Egypt is narrow; the valley between the two ranges is a level plain, and seemed to me to be, at the narrowest point, not more than two hundred furlongs across from the Arabian to the Libyan hills. Above this point Egypt again widens . . . Thus I give credit to those from whom I received this account of Egypt, and am myself, moreover, strongly of the same opinion, since I remarked that the country projects into the sea further than the neighbouring shores, and I observed that there were shells upon the hills, and that salt exuded from the soil to such an extent as even to injure the pyramids; and I noticed also that there is but a single hill in all Egypt where sand is found, namely, the hill above Memphis; and further, I found the country to bear no resemblance either to its borderland Arabia, or to Libya – nay, nor even to Syria, which forms the seaboard of Arabia; but whereas the soil of Libya is, we know, sandy and of a reddish hue, and that of Arabia and Syria inclines to stone and clay, Egypt has a soil that is black and crumbly, as being alluvial and formed of the deposits brought down by the river from Ethiopia.

One fact which I learnt of the priests is to me a strong evidence of the origin of the country. They said that when Moeris was king, the Nile overflowed all Egypt below Memphis, as soon as it rose so little as eight cubits. Now Moeris had not been dead 900 years at the time when I heard this of the priests; yet at the present day, unless the river rise sixteen, or, at the very least, fifteen cubits, it does not overflow the lands . . . With regard to the *sources* of the Nile, I have found no one among all those with whom I have conversed, whether Egyptians, Libyans, or Greeks, who professed to have any knowledge, except a single person. He was the scribe who kept the register of the sacred treasures of Athena in the city of Saïs, and he did not seem to me to be in earnest when he said that he knew them perfectly well. His story was as follows: – 'Between Syênê, a city of the Thebaïs, and Elephantiné, there are' (he said) 'two hills with sharp conical tops; the name of the one is Crophi, of the other, Mophi. Midway between them are the fountains of the Nile, fountains which it is impossible to fathom. Half the water runs northward into Egypt, half to the south towards Ethiopia.' The fountains were known to be unfathomable, he declared, because Psammetichus, an Egyptian king, had made trial of them. He had caused a rope to be made, many thousand fathoms in length, and had sounded the fountain with it, but could find no bottom. By this the scribe gave me to understand, if there was any truth at all in what he said, that in this fountain there are certain strong eddies, and a regurgitation, owing to the force wherewith the water dashes against the mountains, and hence a sounding-line cannot be got to reach the bottom of the spring.

No other information on this head could I obtain from any quarter. All that I succeeded in learning further of the more distant portions of the Nile, by ascending myself as high as Elephantiné, and making inquiries concerning the parts beyond, was the following: – As one advances beyond Elephantiné, the land rises. Hence it is necessary in this part of the river to attach a rope to the boat on each side, as men harness an ox, and so proceed on the journey. If the rope snaps, the vessel is borne away down stream by the force of the current. The navigation continues the same for four days, the river winding greatly, like the Maeander, and the distance traversed amounting to twelve schoenes. Here you come upon a smooth and level plain, where the Nile flows in two branches, round an island called Tachompso. The country above Elephantiné is inhabited by the Ethiopians, who possess one-half of this island, the Egyptians occupying the other. Above the island there is a great lake, the shores of which are inhabited by Ethiopian nomads.

GUSTAVE FLAUBERT

🌶

Letter to Jules Cloquet from Cairo, 15 January 1850

In Cairo, you brush against all the costumes of the Orient, elbow all its peoples; you see the Greek *papá* with his long beard riding his mule, the Albanian soldier in his embroidered jacket, the Copt in his black turban, the Persian in his fur pelisse, the desert Bedouin with his coffee-coloured face walking gravely along enveloped in his white robes.

In Europe we picture the Arab as very serious. Here he is very merry, very artistic in gesticulation and ornamentation. Circumcisions and marriages seem to be nothing but pretexts for rejoicing and music-making. Those are the days when you hear the loud *zagárit* of the Arab women in the streets: swathed in veils and holding their elbows well out as they ride on their donkeys, they resemble nothing so much as black full-moons coming toward you on four-legged somethings. Officialdom is so far removed from the populace that the latter enjoys unlimited freedom – of speech, that is. The 'most extreme excesses of our Press' would give but a feeble idea of the buffooneries that are allowed in the public squares. Here the mountebank approaches the sublime in cynicism. If Boileau thought that Latin words offend chaste sensibilities, what on earth would he have said had he known Arabic! Furthermore, the Arab needs no dragoman to make himself understood: pantomime illustrates his comments. Even animals are made to participate in the obscene symbolism.

Anyone who is a little attentive *re*discovers here much more than he discovers. The seeds of a thousand notions that one carried within oneself grow and become more definite, like so many refreshed memories. Thus, as soon as I landed at Alexandria I saw before me, alive, the anatomy of the Egyptian sculptures: the high shoulders, long torso, thin legs, etc. The dances that we have had performed for us are of too hieratic a character not to have come from the dances of the old Orient, which is always young because nothing changes. Here the Bible is a picture of life today. Do you know that until a few years ago the murderer of an ox was still punished by death, exactly as in the time of Apis? You can see that there is much to enjoy in all this, and plenty of opportunity to utter stupidities about it – something which we abstain from as much as possible.

GUSTAVE FLAUBERT

✎

Letter to Louis Bouilhet, 13 March 1850

At Kena I did something suitable, which I trust will win your approval: we had landed to buy supplies and were walking peacefully and dreamily in the bazaars, inhaling the odour of sandalwood that floated about us, when suddenly, at a turn in the street, we found ourselves in the whores' quarter. Picture to yourself, my friend, five or six curving streets lined with hovels about four feet high, built of dried grey mud. In the doorways, women standing or sitting on straw mats. The negresses had dresses of sky-blue; others were in yellow, in white, in red – loose garments fluttering in the hot wind. Odours of spices. On their bare breasts long necklaces of gold piastres, so that when they move they rattle like carts. They call after you in drawling voices: '*Cawadja, cawadja,*' their white teeth gleaming between their red or black lips, their metallic eyes rolling like wheels. I walked through those streets and walked through them again, giving *baksheesh* to all the women, letting them call me and catch hold of me; they took me around the waist and tried to pull me into their houses – think of all that, with the sun blazing down on it. Well, I abstained. (Young Du Camp did not follow my example.) I abstained deliberately, in order to preserve the sweet sadness of the scene and engrave it deeply in my memory. In this way I went away dazzled, and have remained so. There is nothing more beautiful than these women calling you. If I had gone with any of them, a second picture would have been superimposed on the first and dimmed its splendour.

I haven't always made such sacrifices on the altar of art. At Esna in one day I came five times.

FANNY BURNEY

Journey to Paris

Our passports were examined; and we then went to the port, and, the sea being perfectly smooth, were lifted from the quay to the deck of our vessel with as little difficulty as we could have descended from a common chair to the ground.

The calm which caused our slow passage and our sickness, was now favourable, for it took us into the port of Calais so close and even with the quay, that we scarcely accepted even a hand to aid us from the vessel to the shore.

The quay was lined with crowds of people, men, women, and children, and certain amphibious females, who might have passed for either sex, or anything else in the world, except what they really were, European women! Their men's hats, men's jackets, and men's shoes; their burnt skins, and most savage-looking petticoats, hardly reaching, nay, not reaching their knees, would have made me instantly believe any account I could have heard of their being just imported from the wilds of America.

The vessel was presently filled with men, who, though dirty and mean, were so civil and gentle, that they could not displease, and who entered it so softly and quietly, that, neither hearing nor seeing their approach, it seemed as if they had availed themselves of some secret trap-doors through which they had mounted to fill the ship, without sound or bustle, in a single moment. When we were quitting it, however, this tranquillity as abruptly finished, for in an instant a part of them rushed round me, one demanding to carry Alex! another Adrienne, another seizing my écritoire, another my arm, and some one, I fear, my parasol, as I have never been able to find it since.

We were informed we must not leave the ship till Monsieur le Commissaire arrived to carry us, I think, to the municipality of Calais to show our passports. Monsieur le Commissaire, in white with some red trappings, soon arrived, civilly hastening himself quite out of breath to save us from waiting. We then mounted the quay, and I followed the rest of the passengers, who all followed the commissary, accompanied by two men carrying the two children, and two more carrying, one my écritoire, and the other insisting on conducting its owner. The quality of people that surrounded and walked with us, surprised me; and their decency, their silence, their quietness astonished me. To fear them was impossible, even in entering France with all the formed fears hanging upon its recent though past horrors.

But on coming to the municipality, I was, I own, extremely ill at ease, when upon our gouvernante's desiring me to give the commissary my passport, as the rest of the passengers had done, and my answering it was in my écritoire, she exclaimed, '*Vite! vite! cherchez-le, ou vous serez arrêtée!*' You may be sure I was quick enough! – or at least tried to be so, for my fingers presently trembled, and I could hardly put in the key.

In the hall to which we now repaired, our passports were taken and deposited, and we had new ones drawn up and given us in their stead. On quitting this place we were accosted by a new crowd, all however as gentle, though not as silent, as our first friends, who recommended various hotels to us, one begging we would go to Grandsire, another to Duroc, another to Meurice – and this last prevailed with the gouvernante, whom I regularly followed, not from preference, but from the singular horror my otherwise

123

worthy and well-bred old lady manifested, when, by being approached by the children, her full round coats risked the danger of being modernized into the flimsy, falling drapery of the present day.

At Meurice's our goods were entered, and we heard that they would be examined at the custom-house in the afternoon. We breakfasted, and the crowd of fees which were claimed by the captain, steward, sailors, carriers, and heaven knows who besides, are inconceivable. I gave whatever they asked, from ignorance of what was due, and from fear of offending those of whose extent still less of whose use of power I could form no judgment. I was the only one in this predicament; the rest refusing or disputing every demand. They all, but us, went out to walk; but I stayed to write to my dearest father, to Mrs Lock, and my expecting mate.

We were all three too much awake by the new scene to try for any repose, and the hotel windows sufficed for our amusement till dinner; and imagine, my dearest sir, how my repast was seasoned, when I tell you that, as soon as it began, a band of music came to the window and struck up 'God save the King'. I can never tell you what a pleased emotion was excited in my breast by this sound on a shore so lately hostile.

GRAHAM GREENE

❧

'The Border'

The border means more than a customs house, a passport officer, a man with a gun. Over there everything is going to be different; life is never going to be quite the same again after your passport has been stamped and you find yourself speechless among the money-changers. The man seeking scenery imagines strange woods and unheard-of mountains; the romantic believes that the women over the border will be more beautiful and complaisant than those at home; the unhappy man imagines at least a different hell; the suicidal traveller expects the death he never finds. The atmosphere of the border – it is like starting over again; there is something about it like a good confession: poised for a few happy moments between sin and sin. When people die on the border they call it 'a happy death'.

The money-changers' booths in Laredo formed a whole street, running downhill to the international bridge; then they ran uphill on the other side into Mexico, just the same but a little shabbier. What makes a tourist choose one money-changer rather than another? The same prices were chalked up all the way down to the slow brown river – '3.50 pesos for a dollar'; '3.50 pesos for a dollar'. Perhaps they look at the faces, but the faces were all the same too – half-caste faces.

I had imagined a steady stream of tourist cars going across from America on this side into Mexico over there, but there wasn't one. Life seemed to pile up like old cans and boots against a breakwater; you were part of the silt yourself. A man in San Antonio had said I'd be sure to find a car going down, and an agent near the bridge-head said that was right – he knew for a fact that there was a Mexican driving down from San Antonio ('in a fine German car') who would give me a seat to Mexico City for a few dollars. I waited and waited and of course he never turned up; I don't think he even existed, though why they should have wanted to keep me on *their* side of the river I don't know. They weren't getting any money out of me.

Every half-hour I walked down to the river bank and looked at Mexico; it looked just the same as where I was – I could see the money-changers' booths running uphill through the heat and a kind of mass of people near the bridge-head – the silt washing up on their side of the breakwater too. I could imagine them saying over there: 'There's an American going from Monterey to New York in a fine German car. He'll give you a seat for a few dollars;' and people like me were waiting on the other side, staring across the Rio Grande at the money-changers and thinking: 'That's the United States', waiting for a traveller who didn't exist at all. It was like looking at yourself in a mirror.

D. H. LAWRENCE

from *Mornings in Mexico*

One says Mexico: one means, after all, one little town away
South in the Republic: and in this little town, one rather
crumbly adobe house built round two sides of a garden
patio: and of this house, one spot on the deep, shady
verandah facing inwards to the trees, where there are an
onyx table and three rocking-chairs and one little wooden
chair, a pot with carnations, and a person with a pen. We
talk so grandly, in capital letters, about Morning in Mexico.
All it amounts to is one little individual looking at a bit of
sky and trees, then looking down at the page of his exercise
book.

It is a pity we don't always remember this. When books
come out with grand titles, like *The Future of America* or *The
European Situation*, it's a pity we don't immediately visualize
a thin or a fat person, in a chair or in bed, dictating to a
bob-haired stenographer or making little marks on paper
with a fountain pen.

Still, it is morning, and it is Mexico. The sun shines. But
then, during the winter, it always shines. It is pleasant to sit
out of doors and write, just fresh enough, and just warm
enough. But then it is Christmas next week, so it ought to be
just right.

There is a little smell of carnations, because they are the
nearest thing. And there is a resinous smell of ocote wood,
and a smell of coffee, and a faint smell of leaves, and of

Morning, and even of Mexico. Because when all is said and done, Mexico has a faint, physical scent of her own, as each human being has. And this is a curious, inexplicable scent, in which there are resin and perspiration and sun-burned earth and urine among other things.

And cocks are still crowing. The little mill where the natives have their corn ground is puffing rather languidly. And because some women are talking in the entrance-way, the two tame parrots in the trees have started to whistle.

The parrots, even when I don't listen to them, have an extraordinary effect on me, They make my diaphragm convulse with little laughs, almost mechanically. They are a quite commonplace pair of green birds, with bits of bluey red, and round, disillusioned eyes, and heavy, overhanging noses. But they listen intently. And they reproduce. The pair whistle now like Rosalino, who is sweeping the *patio* with a twig broom; and yet it is so unlike him, to be whistling full vent, when any of us is around, that one looks at him to see. And the moment one sees him, with his black head bent rather drooping and hidden as he sweeps, one laughs.

The parrots whistle exactly like Rosalino, only a little more so. And this little-more-so is extremely, sardonically funny. With their sad old long-jowled faces and their flat disillusioned eyes, they reproduce Rosalino and a little-more-so without moving a muscle. And Rosalino, sweeping the *patio* with his twig broom, scraping the tittering leaves into little heaps, covers himself more and more with the cloud of his own obscurity. He doesn't rebel. He is powerless. Up goes the wild, sliding Indian whistle into the morning, very powerful, with an immense energy seeming to drive behind it. And always, always a little more than lifelike.

Then they break off into a cackling chatter, and one knows they are shifting their clumsy legs, perhaps hanging on with their beaks and clutching with their cold, slow claws, to climb to a higher bough, like rather raggedy green buds climbing to the sun. And suddenly, the penetrating, demonish mocking voices:

'Perro! Oh, Perro! Perr-rro! Oh, Perr-rro! Perro!'

They are imitating somebody calling the dog. *Perro* means dog. But that any creature should be able to pour such a suave, prussic-acid sarcasm over the voice of a human being calling a dog, is incredible. One's diaphragm chuckles involuntarily. And one thinks: *Is it possible?* Is it possible that we are so absolutely, so innocently, so *ab ovo* ridiculous?

And not only is it possible, it is patent.

ANTONIO PIGAFETTA

A 'Giant' on The Shores of Patagonia

One day, without anyone expecting it, we saw a giant, who was on the shore of the sea, quite naked, and was dancing and leaping and singing, and whilst singing he put the sand and dust on his head. Our captain [Magellan] sent one of his men towards him, whom he charged to sing and leap like the other to reassure him, and show him friendship. This he did, and immediately the sailor led this giant to a little island where the captain was waiting for him; and when he was before us he began to be astonished, and to be afraid, and he raised one finger on high, thinking that we came from heaven. He was so tall that the tallest of us only came up to his waist; however he was well built. He had a large face, painted red all round, and his eyes also were painted yellow around them, and he had two hearts painted on his cheeks; he had but little hair on his head, and it was painted white. When he was brought before the captain he was clothed with the skin of a certain beast, which skin was very skilfully sewed. This beast has its head and ears of the size of a mule, and the neck and body of the fashion of a camel, the legs of a deer, and the tail like that of a horse, and it neighs like a horse. There is a great quantity of these animals in this same place. This giant had his feet covered with the skin of this animal in the form of shoes, and he carried in his hand a short and thick bow, with a thick cord made of the gut of the said beast, with a bundle of cane arrows, which were not very long, and were feathered like ours, but they had no iron at the end, though they had at the end some small white and black cut stones, and these arrows were like those which the Turks use. The captain caused food and drink to be given to this giant, then they showed him some things, amongst others, a steel mirror. When the giant saw his likeness in it, he was greatly terrified, leaping backwards, and made three or four of our men fall down.

After that the captain gave him two bells, a mirror, a comb, and a chaplet of beads, and sent him back on shore, having him accompanied by four armed men. One of the companions of this giant, who would never come to the ship, on seeing the other coming back with our people, came forward and ran to where the other giants dwelled. These came one after the other all naked, and began to leap and sing, raising one finger to heaven, and showing to our people a certain white powder made of the roots of herbs, which they kept in earthen pots, and they made signs that they lived on that, and that they had nothing else to eat than this powder. Therefore our people made them signs to come to the ship and that they would help them to carry their bundles. Then these men came, who carried only their bows in their hands; but their wives came after them laden like donkeys, and carried their goods. These women are not as tall as the men, but they are very sufficiently large. When we saw them we were all amazed and astonished, for they had the breasts half an ell long, and had their faces painted, and were dressed like the men. But they wore a small skin before them to cover themselves. They brought with them four of those little beasts of which they make their clothing, and they led them with a cord in the manner of dogs coupled together.

CHIEF BUFFALO CHILD LONG LANCE

❧

'The White Man'

We travelled along the Namaka until we came to the
foothills of the Rockies, and here we came upon the
Suksiseoketuk Indians – the Rocky Mountain Band of
Assiniboines – whose hunting-grounds were up there in the
foothill country. Their chief, Chief Travels-Against-The-
Wind, asked us who we were. Our chief said:

'We are roving *Seeha-sapa* from the plains, whose only
enemy is the *Okotoks Isahpo* – the Rock Band of Crows.'

'*Ha-h! Neena-washtay – washtaydo. Amba wastaytch, Seeha-sapa*! – Oh! Very good – exceptionally good. Howdy do
Blackfeet,' said the Suksiseoketuk chief.

Then he told our chief to tell his tribesmen to get off their
ponies and sit down and he would have the Suksiseoketuk
women make us some of the white man's *minne-seeha* –
'black water', or tea. And the chief said that while we were
drinking of it he would tell us about the white man.

We had never had tea before, and we youngsters did not
like it; it was bitter. The chief said that the Hudson's Bay
Company had traded it for some of their skins – and they
seemed to like this tea. Our old people liked it, too.

But we boys were very interested in what the chief told us
about the white man. He told us to beware of his food; as it
would make our teeth come out. He told us about the bread
and the sweets which the white man ate, and he pulled up
his upper lip and said:

'*Wambadahka* – Behold – my teeth are good, and so are the teeth of all our old people; but behold,' he said, walking over to a young boy and pulling up his lip, 'behold, these teeth of the young people are not good – too much white man's food. Our people, like yours, never used to die until they were over a hundred years old. Now, since we started to eat that white man's food we are sick all of the time. We keep getting worse and soon it will kill us all.'

And then the chief reached up and took hold of a shock of his hair at the top of his head, and he said:

'*Payheeh* – hair – the white man has none of this on top of his head. The crown of his head is as slick as the nose of a buffalo. Every time the Indian eats he wipes grease into his hair. White man wash it all out with bad medicine – soap – take all grease out and make all of his hair drop off. Swap your buffalo robes for the white man's blankets and gunpowder, but take not of his food,' said the chief, 'nor of his "bad medicine" for washing your hair.'

⋅ The next day we started north, accompanied by fifty of the Suksiseoketuk warriors. We travelled for six days, keeping always to the edge of the foothills. On the sixth day the Suksiseoketuks told us to pitch our camp at a point we had reached late in the afternoon, and they would send over a messenger to tell the white people at the trading post that we were there to see them.

After we had pitched our camp, several of our warriors went out to see if they could find some otter, which were plentiful in that part of the northland. While they were out they came upon a cabin, and they saw six long-haired people with light skin, going in and out of this place. Our warriors sat down and watched them and tried to figure out what they were; they had never seen any people like them before. They were not Indians and they were not white men; so one of our warriors, Big Darkness, said that they must be the white man's woman – their wives – white women! They had never seen any white women before; so they all agreed that that must be what they were.

But when they came back to camp and told the others about it, another of our warriors, Sun Calf, who had seen the women, changed his mind and said that he did not believe they were white women after all; they were 'some other kind of people', he said.

This started an argument which became so heated that our chief was afraid that it would lead to a fight. So he said the best way to settle the dispute was for the two warriors to put up a bet, and then go over and capture one of the 'strange beings' and bring it back, and the camp would decide what they were.

The men led out five ponies each and bet them on their respective beliefs. And when darkness came ten of our warriors, including Big Darkness and Sun Calf, crept over to the shack and overpowered one of the 'strange beings' and brought it back.

When they returned to our camp, we were waiting around a big fire singing, so that the disturbance would not attract the trading post. They led a very scared-looking 'being' to the edge of the fire, and Big Darkness exclaimed to the throng:

'Now look. Is it not a woman?'

Half of the tribe believed that it was a woman, and the other half said that it was not. The confusion of the argument which followed grew so noisy that it awoke some of the Suksiseoketuk warriors who had their camp about a hundred yards away, and they came over to see what was going on.

They stopped and listened for a moment, and then they began to laugh. They laughed for a long time before they would tell us what they were laughing at. And then one of them said:

'Inexperienced Blackfeet! It is neither a white woman nor any kind of being that you have ever seen before. It is a man from across the *Minne-Tonka*,' and he waved his arm towards the Pacific Ocean.

It was a Chinaman! One of the Chinese employed as cooks by some white prospectors.

SAMUEL JOHNSON

At Loch Ness, 1773

We were now to bid farewell to the luxury of travelling, and
to enter a country upon which perhaps no wheel has ever
rolled. We could indeed have used our post-chaise one day
longer, along the military road to Fort Augustus, but we
could have hired no horses beyond Inverness, and we were
not so sparing of ourselves, as to lead them, merely that we
might have one day longer the indulgence of a carriage.

At Inverness therefore we procured three horses for
ourselves and a servant, and one more for our baggage,
which was no very heavy load. We found in the course of
our journey the convenience of having disencumbered
ourselves, by laying aside whatever we could spare; for it is
not to be imagined without experience, how in climbing
crags, and treading bogs, and winding through narrow and
obstructed passages, a little bulk will hinder, and a little
weight will burthen; or how often a man that has pleased
himself at home with his own resolution, will, in the hour of
darkness and fatigue, be content to leave behind him every
thing but himself.

We took two Highlanders to run beside us, partly to shew us
the way, and partly to take back from the sea-side the
horses, of which they were the owners. One of them was a
man of great liveliness and activity, of whom his companion said that he would tire any horse in Inverness. Both of

them were civil and ready-handed. Civility seems part of the national character of Highlanders . . .

Most of the day's journey was very pleasant. The day, though bright, was not hot; and the appearance of the country, if I had not seen the Peak, would have been wholly new. We went upon a surface so hard and level, that we had little care to hold the bridle, and were therefore at full leisure for contemplation. On the left were high and steep rocks shaded with birch, the hardy native of the North, and covered with fern or heath. On the right the limpid waters of Lough Ness were beating their bank, and waving their surface by a gentle agitation. Beyond them were rocks sometimes covered with verdure, and sometimes towering in horrid nakedness. Now and then we espied a little corn-field, which served to impress more strongly the general barrenness.

Lough Ness is about twenty-four miles long, and from one mile to two miles broad. It is remarkable that Boethius, in his description of Scotland, gives it twelve miles of breadth. When historians or geographers exhibit false accounts of places far distant, they may be forgiven, because they can tell but what they are told; and that their accounts exceed the truth may be justly supposed, because most men exaggerate to others, if not to themselves: but Boethius lived at no great distance; if he never saw the lake, he must have been very incurious, and if he had seen it, his veracity yielded to very slight temptations . . .

Near the way, by the water-side, we espied a cottage. This was the first Highland hut that I had seen; and as our business was with life and manners, we were willing to visit it. To enter a habitation without leave, seems to be not considered here as rudeness or intrusion. The old laws of hospitality still give this licence to a stranger.

A hut is constructed with loose stones, ranged for the most part with some tendency to circularity. It must be placed where the wind cannot act upon it with violence, because it has no cement; and where the water will run easily away, because it has no floor but the naked ground. The wall, which is commonly about six feet high, declines from the perpendicular a little inward. Such rafters as can be procured are then raised for a roof, and covered with heath, which makes a strong and warm thatch, kept from flying off by ropes of twisted heath, of which the ends, reaching from the centre of the thatch to the top of the wall, are held firm by the weight of a large stone. No light is admitted but at the entrance and through a hole in the thatch, which gives vent to the smoke. This hole is not directly over the fire, lest the rain should extinguish it; and the smoke therefore naturally fills the place before it escapes. Such is the general structure of the houses in which one of the nations of this opulent and powerful island has been hitherto content to live. Huts however are not more uniform than palaces; and this which we were inspecting was very far from one of the meanest, for it was divided into several apartments; and its inhabitants possessed such property as a pastoral poet might exalt into riches.

When we entered, we found an old woman boiling goats-flesh in a kettle. She spoke little English, but we had interpreters at hand; and she was willing enough to display her whole system of economy. She has five children, of which none are yet gone from her. The eldest, a boy of thirteen, and her husband, who is eighty years old, were at work in the wood. Her two next sons were gone to Inverness to buy meal, by which oatmeal is always meant. Meal she considered as expensive food, and told us, that in Spring, when the goats gave milk, the children could live without it. She is mistress of sixty goats, and I saw many kids in an enclosure at the end of her house. She had also some poultry. By the lake we saw a potatoe-garden, and a small spot of ground on which stood four shucks, containing each twelve sheaves of barley. She has all this from the labour of their own hands, and for what is necessary to be bought, her kids and her chickens are sent to market.

With the true pastoral hospitality, she asked us to sit

down and drink whisky. She is religious, and though the kirk is four miles off, probably eight English miles, she goes thither every Sunday. We gave her a shilling, and she begged snuff; for snuff is the luxury of a Highland cottage.

JAMES BOSWELL

from *Journal of a Tour to the Hebrides*

20 August 1773

About eleven at night we arrived at Montrose. We found but a sorry inn, where I myself saw another waiter put a lump of sugar with his fingers into Dr Johnson's lemonade, for which he called him 'Rascal!' . . .

He was angry at me for proposing to carry lemons with us to Sky, that he might be sure to have his lemonade. 'Sir,' said he. 'I do not wish to be thought that feeble man who cannot do without any thing. Sir, it is very bad manners to carry provisions to any man's house, as if he could not entertain you. To an inferior, it is oppressive; to a superior, it is insolent.'

EDWARD LEAR

from *Journals of a Landscape Painter*
in Calabria

No wilder, nor more extraordinary place than Palizzi can
well greet artist eye. Leaving P——— to finish a drawing I
went forward to seek some shelter against the heat, and,
reaching the castle, soon found myself in the midst of its
ruined area, where, though full of incidental picturesque-
ness – namely, a cottage, a pergola, seven large pigs, a blind
man, and a baby, I could get no information as to the
whereabouts of the taverna; until alarmed by the lively
remonstrances of the pigs, there appeared a beautifully fair
girl who directed me down to the middle of the town: the
light hair, and Grecian traits, like those of the women of
Gaeta, seemed to recall the daughters of Magna Graecia.

The streets of Palizzi, through which no Englishman
perhaps had as yet descended, were swarming with perfectly naked, berry-brown children, and before I reached the
taverna I could hardly make my way through the gathering
crowd of astonished mahogany Cupids. The taverna was
but a single dark room, its walls hung with portraits of little
saints, and its furniture a very filthy bed with a crimson
velvet gold-fringed canopy, containing an unclothed oph-
thalmic baby, an old cat, and a pointer dog; all the rest of
the chamber being loaded with rolls of linen, guns, gourds,
pears, hats, glass tumblers, puppies, jugs, sieves, etc.; still it
was a better resting-place than the hut at Condufóri,

inasmuch as it was free from many intruders. Until P———came, and joined with me in despatching a feeble dinner of eggs, figs and cucumber, wine and snow, I sate exhibited and displayed for the benefit of the landlord, his wife, and family, who regarded me with unmingled amazement, saying perpetually, 'O donde siete?' – 'O che fai?' – 'O chi sei?'* And, indeed, the passage of a stranger through these outlandish places is so unusual an occurrence, that on no principle but one can the aborigines account for your appearance. 'Have you *no* rocks, *no* towns, *no* trees in your own country? Are you not rich? Then what *can* you wish *here*? – *here*, in this place of poverty and incommodo? What *are* you doing? Where *are* you going?' You might talk for ever; but you could not convince them you are not a political agent sent to spy out the nakedness of the land, and masking the intentions of your government under the thin veil of portraying scenes, in which they see no novelty, and take no delight.

*Oh where do you come from? – Oh what *are* you going to do? – Oh who *can* you be?

THOMAS MOORE

♥

With Byron in Italy

He [Byron] had ordered dinner from some *tratteria*, and while waiting its arrival – as well as that of Mr Alexander Scott, whom he had invited to join us – we stood out on the balcony, in order that, before the daylight was quite gone, I might have some glimpses of the scene which the Canal presented. Happening to remark, in looking up at the clouds, which were still bright in the west, that 'what had struck me in Italian sunsets was that peculiar rosy hue –' I had hardly pronounced the word 'rosy', when Lord Byron, clapping his hand on my mouth, said, with a laugh, 'Come, d—n it, Tom, *don't* be poetical.'

WILLIAM SHAKESPEARE

from *Othello*

OTHELLO Her father loved me, oft invited me,
  Still questioned me the story of my life
  From year to year, the battles, sieges, fortunes
  That I have passed.
  I ran it through even from my boyish days
  To th' very moment that he bade me tell it,
  Wherein I spoke of most disastrous chances,
  Of moving accidents by flood and field,
  Of hair-breadth scapes i'th' imminent deadly breach,
  Of being taken by the insolent foe
  And sold to slavery, of my redemption thence,
  And portance in my traveller's history,
  Wherein of antres vast and deserts idle,
  Rough quarries, rocks, and hills whose heads touch
    heaven,
  It was my hint to speak. Such was my process,
  And of the cannibals that each other eat,
  The Anthropophagi, and men whose heads
  Do grow beneath their shoulders. These things to hear
  Would Desdemona seriously incline,
  But still the house affairs would draw her thence,
  Which ever as she could with haste dispatch
  She'd come again, and with a greedy ear
  Devour up my discourse; which I observing,
  Took once a pliant hour, and found good means

To draw from her a prayer of earnest heart
That I would all my pilgrimage dilate,
Whereof by parcels she had something heard,
But not intentively. I did consent,
And often did beguile her of her tears
When I did speak of some distressful stroke
That my youth suffered. My story being done,
She gave me for my pains a world of kisses.
She swore in faith 'twas strange, 'twas passing strange,
'Twas pitiful, 'twas wondrous pitiful.
She wished she had not heard it, yet she wished
That heaven had made her such a man. She thanked me,
And bade me, if I had a friend that loved her,
I should but teach him how to tell my story,
And that would woo her. Upon this hint I spake.
She loved me for the dangers I had passed,
And I loved her that she did pity them.
This only is the witchcraft I have used.

JEAN RHYS

❦

from *Wide Sargasso Sea*

The boy brought the horses to a large stone and I saw Antoinette coming from the hut. The sun blazed out and steam rose from the green behind us. Amélie took her shoes off, tied them together and hung them round her neck. She balanced her small basket on her head and swung away as easily as the porters. We mounted, turned a corner and the village was out of sight. A cock crowed loudly and I remembered the night before which we had spent in the town. Antoinette had a room to herself, she was exhausted. I lay awake listening to cocks crowing all night, then got up very early and saw the women with trays covered with white cloths on their heads going to the kitchen. The woman with small, hot loaves for sale, the woman with cakes, the woman with sweets. In the street another called '*Bon sirop, bon sirop*', and I felt peaceful.

The road climbed upward. On one side the wall of green, on the other a steep drop to the ravine below. We pulled up and looked at the hills, the mountains and the blue-green sea. There was a soft, warm wind blowing but I understood why the porter had called it a wild place. Not only wild but menacing. Those hills would close in on you.

'What an extreme green,' was all I could say, and thinking of Emile calling to the fisherman and the sound of his voice, I asked about him.

'They take short cuts. They will be at Granbois long before we are.'

Everything is too much, I felt as I rode wearily after her. Too much blue, too much purple, too much green. The flowers too red, the mountains too high, the hills too near. And the woman is a stranger. Her pleading expression annoys me. I have not bought her, she has bought me, or so she thinks. I looked down at the coarse mane of the horse . . . Dear Father. The thirty thousand pounds have been paid to me without question or condition. No provision made for her (that must be seen to). I have a modest competence now. I will never be a disgrace to you or to my dear brother, the son you love. No begging letters, no mean requests. None of the furtive shabby manoeuvres of a younger son. I have sold my soul or you have sold it, and after all is it such a bad bargain? The girl is thought to be beautiful, she is beautiful. And yet . . .

Meanwhile the horses jogged along a very bad road. It was getting cooler. A bird whistled, a long, sad note. 'What bird is that?' She was too far ahead and did not hear me. The bird whistled again. A mountain bird. Shrill and sweet. A very lonely sound.

She stopped and called, 'Put your coat on now.' I did so and realized that I was no longer pleasantly cool but cold in my sweat-soaked shirt.

We rode on again, silent in the slanting afternoon sun, the wall of trees on one side, a drop on the other. Now the sea was a serene blue, deep and dark.

We came to a little river. 'This is the boundary of Granbois.' She smiled at me. It was the first time I had seen her smile simply and naturally. Or perhaps it was the first time I had felt simple and natural with her. A bamboo spout jutted from the cliff, the water coming from it was silver blue. She dismounted quickly, picked a large shamrock-shaped leaf to make a cup, and drank. Then she picked another leaf, folded it and brought it to me. 'Taste. This is mountain water.' Looking up smiling, she might have been any pretty English girl and to please her I drank. It was cold, pure and sweet, a beautiful colour against the thick green leaf.

She said, 'After this we go down then up again. Then we are there.'

Next time she spoke she said, 'The earth is red here, do you notice?'

'It's red in parts of England too.'

'Oh, England, England,' she called back mockingly, and the sound went on and on like a warning I did not choose to hear.

Soon the road was cobblestoned and we stopped at a flight of stone steps. There was a large screw pine to the left and to the right what looked like an imitation of an English summer house – four wooden posts and a thatched roof. She dismounted and ran up the steps. At the top a badly cut, coarse-grained lawn and at the end of the lawn a shabby white house. 'Now you are at Granbois.'

BOB DYLAN

'Black Diamond Bay'

Up on the white verandah
she wears a necktie and a
Panama hat.
Her passport shows a face
from another time and place,
she looks nothing like that.
And all of the remnants of her
recent past are
scattered in the wild wind.
She walks across the marble floor
where a voice from the gambling-room is
calling her to come on in.
She smiles, walks the other way
as the last ship sails and the moon fades away
from Black Diamond Bay.

As the morning light breaks open
the Greek comes down and he asks for rope and
a pen that will write.
Pardon Monsieur, the desk-clerk says
And carefully removes his fez
Am I hearing you right?
And as the yellow fog is lifting
the Greek is quickly
heading for the second floor.

She passes him on the spiral staircase
thinking he's the
Soviet ambassador.
She stops to speak but he walks away
as the storm clouds rise and the palm branches sway
on Black Diamond Bay.

A soldier sits beneath the fan
doing business with a tiny man
who sells him a ring.
Lightning strikes, the lights blow out,
The desk-clerk wakes, he begins to shout:
Can you see anything?
Then the Greek appears on the second floor
in his bare feet with a
rope around his neck,
while the loser in the gambling-room
lights up a candle, says:
Open up another deck.
But the dealer says: Attendez-vous s'il vous plaît
as the rain beats down and the cranes fly away
from Black Diamond Bay.

The desk-clerk heard the woman laugh
as he looked around in the aftermath
and the soldier got tough.
He tried to grab the woman's hand,
he said: Here's a ring, it cost a grand.
She said: That ain't enough.
Then she ran upstairs to pack her bags
while a horse-drawn taxi
waited at the kerb.
She passed the door which the Greek had locked
where a handwritten sign said:
Do Not Disturb.
She knocked on it anyway
as the sun went down and the music did play
On Black Diamond Bay.

I've got to talk to someone quick!
But the Greek said; Go away! and he kicked
the chair to the floor.
He hung there from the chandelier,
she cried: Help! There's danger near,
Please open up the door.
Then the volcano erupted and the lava flowed down
from the mountain high above.
The soldier and the tiny man were
crouched in the corner
Thinking of forbidden love.
The desk-clerk said: It happens every day!
As the stars fell down and the moon fades away
From Black Diamond Bay.

As the island slowly sank
the loser finally broke the bank
in the gambling-room.
The dealer said: It's too late now,
you can take your money but I don't know how
you'll spend it in the tomb.
The tiny man bit the soldier's ear
As the floor caved in and the
Boiler in the basement blew.
Well, she's out on the balcony
where a stranger tells her:
My darling je vous aime beaucoup.
She sheds a tear and then begins to pray
as the land burns on and the smoke drifts away
From Black Diamond Bay.

I was sitting home alone one night
in LA watching old Kronkite
on the seven o'clock news.
Seems there was an earthquake there
Left nothing but a Panama hat and a
pair of old Greek shoes.

Didn't seem like much was happening
so I turned it off and
went to grab another beer.
Seems like every time you turn around
there's another hard luck story
that you're gonna hear,
and there's really nothing anyone can say
and I never did plan to go anyway
to Black Diamond Bay.

CHARLES NICHOLL

❧

from *The Fruit Palace*

The Fruit Palace was always open and never crowded. People drifted in off the street, to trade a bit of gossip and rest from the weight of the sun. In the evenings a few dock-workers might come in for a game of *veinte y una*, with much shouting and slapping down of cards and tossing back of rum. I think Julio, who owned and ran the Fruit Palace, actually preferred business slow. He had dreams of getting rich, he had complex schemes for getting rich, but they were quite divorced from his day-to-day life. Whisking *jugos* was something to do while he waited for the big one to turn up. 'With a little bit of sweet and a little bit of sour,' he said, 'a man is happy.' . . .

With his black stubble, bad teeth, sideburns and faded check shirts, Julio had the typical look of the Colombian *criollo*, the mixed Spanish-Indian type that forms the majority of the country's people. But he had something else – a certain finesse, a dapperness of manner and philosophy. His pointed nose and thick, slightly twirled moustache gave him an oddly *belle époque* air, a minor French dandy somehow adrift down a South American back-street.

Julio's contribution to Santa Marta's black economy was a little modest dealing in emeralds. His father had been an *esmeraldero*, first an emerald miner at Coscuez and then a small-time dealer. Some people have a way with animals: Julio had a way with emeralds. He always had a small consignment on the go, and whenever a new gringo face turned up at the Fruit Palace, it was not long before the talk was steered round to the fabulous virtues of the Colombian gem emerald, *la más famosa en el mundo*. Out would come the little fold of tissue paper, with a pair of Muzo stones or a thimbleful of uncut *canutillos* winking inside. He would rock a stone gently in his palm, like a tiny dice. '*Mire, mire, el fuego verde!*' Look at the green fire in it. His prices were always good, even by black market standards. I wondered if he sometimes sold fakes – he certainly spoke expertly about counterfeiting: rock candy, vanadium, doublets and triplets, and so on – but it wouldn't have done to ask him.

Also living at the Fruit Palace was a girl called Miriam, who did the cooking and the cleaning. Julio had a wife and a little daughter, but they were somewhere else for a while – the vagueness was Julio's – and in the meantime he was sharing his bed with Miriam. She was a plump, moody Caquetana girl in her twenties. She wore tight skirts and a man's wrist-watch. As she worked she rendered current hit songs in a tuneless, hissing kind of whistle – her favourite was a tear-jerker entitled '*Volver Volver Volver*'. She was no great beauty, but like Lily in the song she had that certain flash every time she smiled. She flirted slyly with all the gringos. She visited me in my dreams, her breasts syncopating softly as they did when she danced to the songs on the radio. The quiet glint of machismo in Julio's eye was enough to keep it at that.

There was a small back room behind the café which Julio rented out – this was the *residencias* advertised on the sign outside. I had stumbled into the café one day for a beer, straight off the train from Barrancabermeja, a fifteen-hour haul across the Magdalena plains. The room was vacant. Too tired to look for a hotel, I took it for the night. The profound nonchalance of Santa Marta stole over me, and I was still there three months later. The bed had once belonged to Julio's grandmother and had a carved cedarwood headboard of which he was very proud, but it was bone-hard to lie on, and after a while I slept in the hammock out in the yard. When the tiny rent Julio charged for the room grew too onerous, I actually rented the hammock off him for something like 10 pesos a night. I kept my belongings in a large, rusty parrot-cage, procured by Julio for this purpose. I shared the yard with a small contingent of animals. Down at the end by the kitchen lived the hen, immured by night in its miniature shack of old fruit boxes. There was a guard dog pacing on the neighbour's roof, there were rats beneath the concrete walkway, and there was the cockroach – one of many, but definitely *the* cockroach, sleek and fat and shiny brown as a conker.

Julio was delighted with this new arrangement. It had the magic smack of something for nothing. I paid less, he got more, the back room now being free for other gringos – or possibly even *gringuitas* – to fill . . .

When I think now of the Fruit Palace I remember especially the sweet-scented nights. Julio always bought his fruit over-ripe. This was both cheaper and better for making *jugos*, yet another instance of those secret financial harmonies he loved to observe. The musk of sweating tropical fruit pervaded the café. By day it had to compete with the oily aromas of Miriam's cuisine, but at night, swaying in my hammock in the yard, the sweet smell of corruption lay over me like a blanket.

The nights were filled with noises, accordions duelling down in the dockside bars, dogs barking across the low roofs, trucks gunning their engines ready for the long haul south. The dockland seemed to buzz right around the yard walls, delicious and dangerous, a faint periphery of menace like in the nights of childhood. Even in the dead of night, after all the jacks were in their boxes and even the animals were asleep, I would sometimes be woken by a strange concert of groans and squeaks. It was the sound of the sea wind swinging the wooden signboards of the cafés and flophouses down 10th Street. That sudden

154

north-easterly wind, rising off the Caribbean after hours or sometimes days of stillness, was called 'La Loca', the madwoman.

MICHAEL ONDAATJE

Monsoon Notebook (i)

To jungles and gravestones. . . . Reading torn 100-year-old newspaper clippings that come apart in your hands like wet sand, information tough as plastic dolls. Watched leopards sip slowly, watched the crow sitting restless on his branch peering about with his beak open. Have seen the outline of a large fish caught and thrown in the curl of a wave, been where nobody wears socks, where you wash your feet before you go to bed, where I watch my sister who alternatively reminds me of my father, mother and brother. Driven through rainstorms that flood the streets for an hour and suddenly evaporate, where sweat falls in the path of this ballpoint, where the jak fruit rolls across your feet in the back of the jeep, where there are eighteen ways of describing the smell of a durian, where bullocks hold up traffic and steam after the rains.

Have sat down to meals and noticed the fan stir in all the spoons on the dining table. And driven that jeep so often I didn't have time to watch the country slide by thick with event, for everything came directly to me and passed me like snow. The black thick feather of bus exhaust everyone was sentimental against, the man vomiting out of a window, the pig just dead having his hairs burnt off on the Canal Road and old girlfriends from childhood who now towel their kids dry on the other side of the SSC pool, and my watch collecting sea under the glass and gleaming with underwater phosphorus by my bed at night, the inside of both my feet blistering in my first week from the fifteen-cent sandals and the obsessional sarong buying in Colombo, Kandy, Jaffna, Trincomalee, the toddy drink I got subtly smashed on by noon so I slept totally unaware of my dreams. And women and men with naked feet under the dinner table, and after the party the thunderstorm we walked through for five seconds from porch to car, thoroughly soaked and by the time we had driven ten minutes – without headlights which had been stolen that afternoon at the pool – we were dry just from the midnight heat inside the vehicle and the ghosts of steam cruising disorganized off the tarmac roads, and the man sleeping on the street who objected when I woke him each of us talking different languages, me miming a car coming around the corner and hitting him and he, drunk, perversely making me perform this action for him again and again, and I got back into the car fully wet once more and again dry in five miles. And the gecko on the wall waving his tail stiffly his jaws full of dragonfly whose wings symmetrically disappeared into his mouth – darkness filling the almost transparent body, and a yellow enamel-assed spider crossing the bidet and the white rat my daughter claims she saw in the toilet at the Maskeliya tennis club.

I witnessed everything. One morning I would wake and just smell things for the whole day, it was so rich I had to select senses. And still everything moved slowly with the assured fateful speed of a coconut falling on someone's head, like the Jaffna train, like the fan at low speed, like the necessary sleep in the afternoon with dreams blinded by toddy.

❦

Monsoon Notebook (ii)

The bars across the windows did not always work. When bats would invade the house at dusk, the beautiful long-haired girls would rush to the corner of rooms and hide their heads under dresses. The bats suddenly drifting like dark squadrons through the house – for never more than two minutes – arcing into the halls over the uncleared dining room table and out along the verandah where the parents would be sitting trying to capture the cricket scores on the BBC with a shortwave radio.

Wildlife stormed or crept into homes this way. The snake either entered through the bathroom drain for remnants of water or, finding the porch doors open, came in like a king and moved in a straight line through the living room, dining room, the kitchen and servant's quarters, and out the back, as if taking the most civilized short cut to another street in town. Others moved in permanently; birds nested above the fans, the silverfish slid into steamer trunks and photograph albums – eating their way through portraits and wedding pictures. What images of family life they consumed in their minute jaws and took into their bodies no thicker than the pages they ate.

And the animals also on the periphery of rooms and porches, their sounds forever in your ear. During our visit to the jungle, while we slept on the verandah at 3 a.m., night would be suddenly alive with disturbed peacocks. A casual movement from one of them roosting in the trees would waken them all and, so fussing, sounding like branches full of cats, they would weep weep loud into the night.

One evening I kept the tape recorder beside my bed and wakened by them once more out of a deep sleep automatically pressed the machine on to record them. Now, and here, Canadian February, I write this in the kitchen and play that section of cassette to hear not just peacocks but all the noises of the night behind them – inaudible then because they were always there like breath. In this silent room (with its own unheard hum of fridge, fluorescent light) there are these frogs loud as river, gruntings, the whistle of other birds brash and sleepy, but in that night so modest behind the peacocks they were unfocused by the brain – nothing more than darkness, all those sweet loud younger brothers of the night.

EMILY EDEN

❦

On Tour in India, 1837

Mohun ke Serai

We made our first march. The bugle sounds at half-past five to wake us, though the camels perform that ceremony rather earlier, and we set off at six as the clock strikes, for as nobody is allowed to precede the Governor-General, it would be hard upon the camp if we were inexact. The comfort of that rule is inexpressible, as we escape all dust that way . . .

We had a short march – only seven miles and a half. It seems somehow wicked to move 12,000 people with their tents, elephants, camels, horses, trunks, etc., for so little, but there is no help for it. There were a great many robberies in the camp last night. Mrs A. saw a man on his hands and knees creeping through her tent, but she called out, and he ran away without taking anything. Mr B. says, when he and his wife were encamped last year on this spot, which is famous for thieves, they lost everything, even the shawl that was on the bed, and the clothes Mrs B. had left out for the morning wear, and he had to sew her up in a blanket, and drive her to Benares for fresh things . . .

Tamarhabad, Friday 24 November

We marched ten miles to-day. These moves are the most amusing part of the journey; besides the odd native groups, our friends catch us up in their *déshabille* – Mrs A. carrying the baby in an open carriage; Mrs C. with hers fast asleep in a tonjaun; Miss H. on the top of an elephant, pacifying the big boy of the A.'s; Captain D. riding on in a suit of dust-coloured canvas, with a coal-heaver's hat, going as hard as he can, to see that the tent is ready for his wife; Mrs B. carrying Mr B.'s pet cat in her palanquin carriage, with her ayah opposite guarding the parroquet from the cat. Then Giles comes bounding by, in fact, run away with, but apologises for passing us when we arrive, by saying he was going on to take care that tea was ready for us. Then we overtake Captain D.'s dogs, all walking with red great coats on – our dogs all wear coats in the morning; then Chance's servant stalking along, with a great stick in one hand, a shawl draped over his livery, and Chance's nose peeping from under the shawl. F.'s pets travel in her cart.

SPALDING GRAY

❦

from *Swimming to Cambodia*

The next day was a day off. I was staying with Tom Bird because I was trying to save all my money. I had $600 in Thai *bhat* saved up and I figured that if I didn't have a Perfect Moment, I would buy one. So I was staying in Tom's room, we were sharing a room, and on our day off some of us went down to what we had heard was Shangri-La – this most incredible beach.

Now I had thought this was just tourist hype. Every time I've travelled to foreign lands, I've always heard that Shangri-La was just around the corner. So we rented a car and we wound down through the water buffalo and the rice paddies and we came out on this *exquisite* beach. Ooh. No tourists. No flotsam. No jetsam. No cans. No plastic bags. Just water buffalo posing like statues in the mist at the far end of the beach. They were just standing there like they were stuffed. They looked like the Thai entry in the Robert Wilson Olympic Arts event. No ships out there in the Indian Ocean, huge surf – perfect Kodachrome day. The sun hadn't quite broken out and it was bright but not too sunny.

In the distance were some thatched huts where you could go have a little brunch and everyone went over there to order their fresh fish and pineapple and beer, and Ivan and I – like two kids – charged right down into the water. I couldn't believe it, it was body temperature, not too warm, just perfect. You could stay in it all day if you wanted to. I

162

was charging in and out. Ivan went right out, right into the big stuff, but I stayed close to shore.

I was a little nervous about sharks. I have a lot of fears, phobias, and sharks and bears are at the top of the list. In fact, I'm the kind of guy who even checks out swimming pools before I go in. I often think some joker has put a shark in the pool as a practical joke. Also, I still had all my money tucked in my ocean briefs and I couldn't think of a good place to stash it. So I asked Ivan where I should put it and he said, 'Oh, just leave it up on the beach where my cameras are.'

He was a bit of a sadist playing into my masochism, and just as I was about to go into the water he said, 'You know, in Africa when I put my cameras on the beach, the natives would just run right out of the jungle and take them. What are you going to do? Chase them into the jungle. Nooooooo.'

I was looking back at my money and coming and going, and then he said, 'Well Spalding, Spalding, listen man. On our next day off I'm going to teach you how to scuba dive. You'll see fish you've never seen before, you'll have Rapture of the Deep, man, and it will be incredible.'

And I said, 'Oh my God, at last. It's like an initiation. I'll become a man.' I've always wanted to overcome my fears with another guy, you know, skin diving and all that. I've always wanted to try scuba diving but I was afraid of sharks coming up from behind. And now Ivan would help me through my fears and become my scuba-guru.

Ivan said, 'We'll go. And Spalding, you will see fish of all colours – you have never seen anything like it . . . but there are these *Stone Fish* . . . and you don't want to step on one of them Spalding, because you'll be dead in seven seconds. There's no remedy, so wear your sneakers.'

He reminded me of when I was a kid with Kenny Mason. Once when I was sledding in Barrington, Rhode Island, Kenny said, 'There's lions in those woods.' I was seven years old and I believed him. In Barrington, Rhode Island, lions in winter. I ran all the way home, crying.

So I was feeling like that seven-year-old again and I was running in and out of the water like this excited kid because I couldn't believe that I was there in Paradise with Ivan. I didn't think I deserved to be in such a beautiful spot and I'd run out of the water and down the beach to try to get an overview. I'd run down the beach and look back to try to see us there in the surf and each time I'd miss myself and then run back to try to be in it all again. Then down the beach and back and down the beach and back and the third time back . . . Ivan was gone. He had been out in the big surf and he was *gone*, and I thought, oh no, holy shit. He's drowned. Ivan had drowned.

I mean, these things do happen, people do drown. I've read about it, and I read this warning issued by the film which said, 'Don't swim in Phuket.' There had been a number of drownings in recent years from the strong undertow, and the very first thing that went through my head – and it went very fast, the whole thing went very fast – was, of course. He's drowned. Making a film about this much death, some real person actually has to go.

The next thing that went through my head was, it's not my fault! He was suicidal!

And the next thing was, quickly! Find the most responsible man you can. There was no way I was going to swim out in that water, I couldn't get out into that big surf. The first person that came to mind was John Swain, the Paris correspondent for *The London Times*. He had been there when the Khmer Rouge invaded Phnom Penh. He was perhaps the most narcissistic of the reporters, because he had come to Thailand to watch himself be played by Julian Sands. And so I just did it. I just screamed, 'JOHN! JOHN SWAIN! COME QUICKLY, I CAN'T SEE IVAN!'

And everyone dropped their chopsticks and began to run. Some came across the swamp, some ran over the wooden bridge, and the first person to reach the beach was Judy Arthur, the publicist. Judy had been a lifeguard so she had the good sense to run along the high part of the beach. I was down by the dip of the lip of the sea and couldn't see out, and the others were trying to calm me down. My knees were shaking and I was on the verge of throwing up and people were saying, 'Listen, Spalding. Take it easy. Take it easy. He won't drown, he's from South Africa.' I was walking up and down the beach trying to interpret this, trying to figure it out, when Judy Arthur spotted Ivan way out. He had drifted down. Judy saw his head way out there and she called him in.

And I said, 'My God, Ivan! Ivan, listen man, I thought you'd drowned. I really did.'

He said, 'Spalding, I'm really sorry, man. Listen, don't worry about me, I won't drown. I'm from South Africa.'

Then everyone went back to brunch and I said, 'Ivan, don't do that again, please.' After promising he wouldn't, he turned to me and said, 'By the way Spalding, when you called, how many came? Did Judy Freeman come?'

And I said, 'Yes, Judy Freeman came, Judy Arthur came, all the Judies came. Let's go get something to eat.'

THOMAS NASHE

♥

'The Counterfeit Traveller'

All *Italianato* is his talk, and his spade peak is as sharp as if
he had been a pioneer before the walls of Rouen. He will
despise the barbarism of his own country and tell a whole
Legend of Lies of his travels unto Constantinople. If he be
challenged to fight, for his dilatory excuse he objects that it
is not the custom of the Spaniard or the German to look
back to every dog that barks. You shall see a dapper jack,
that hath been but over at Dieppe, wring his face round
about, as a man would stir up a mustard pot, and talk
English through the teeth, like Jacques Scabbed-hams or
Monsieur Mingo de Mousetrap; when, poor slave, he hath
but dipped his bread in wild boar's grease, and come home
again; or been bitten by the shins by a wolf; and saith he
hath adventured upon the barricades of Gurney or Guingan
and fought with the young Guise hand to hand.

WILLIAM WORDSWORTH

'Lucy Poems' II

I travelled among unknown men,
   In lands beyond the sea;
Nor, England! did I know till then
   What love I bore to thee.

'Tis past, that melancholy dream!
   Nor will I quit thy shore
A second time; for still I seem
   To love thee more and more.

Among thy mountains did I feel
   The joy of my desire;
And she I cherished turned her wheel
   Beside an English fire.

Thy mornings showed, thy nights concealed,
   The bowers where Lucy played;
And thine too is the last green field
   That Lucy's eyes surveyed.

US PIONEER SLOGAN

Generally painted on wagons returning to the East

In God we trusted
In Kansas we busted.

FYNES MORYSON

❧

from *Itinerary*

For my part, I thinke variety to be the most pleasing thing in the World, and the best life to be neither contemplative alone, nor active altogether, but mixed of both. God would have made eternall spring, had he not knowne, that the divers seasons would be not onely most profitable to the workes of nature, but also most plesant to his creatures, while the cold Winter makes the temperate Spring more wished. Such is the delight of visiting forraigne Countreys, charming all our sences with most sweet variety.

Let us imitate the Storkes, Swallowes, and Cranes, which like the Nomades yeerely fetch their circuits, and follow the Sunne, without suffering any distemper of the seasons: The fixed Starres have not such power over inferiour bodies, as the wandring Planets. Running water is sweet, but standing pooles stinke: Take away Idlenes, and the bate of all vice is taken away. Men were created to move, as birds to flie; what they learne by nature, that reason joined to nature teacheth us.

In one word, I will say what can be said upon this subject; Every soyle is to a valiant man his own Countrey, as the Sea to the Fishes. We are Citizens of the whole World, yea, not of this World, but of that to come: All our life is a Pilgrimage. God for his onely begotten Sonnes sake, (the true Mercury of Travellers) bring us that are here strangers safely into our true Countrey.

T. S. ELIOT

from 'Little Gidding'

We shall not cease from exploration
And the end of all our exploring
Will be to arrive where we started
And know the place for the first time.

SORYŪ

Postscript to Bashō's *The Narrow Road to the Deep North*

In this little book of travel is included everything under the sky – not only that which is hoary and dry but also that which is young and colourful, not only that which is strong and imposing but also that which is feeble and ephemeral. As we turn every corner of the Narrow Road to the Deep North, we sometimes stand up unawares to applaud and we sometimes fall flat to resist the agonizing pains we feel in the depths of our hearts. There are also times when we feel like taking to the road ourselves, seizing the raincoat lying near by, or times when we feel like sitting down till our legs take root, enjoying the scene we picture before our eyes. Such is the beauty of this little book that it can be compared to the pearls which are said to be made by the weeping mermaids in the far-off sea. What a travel it is indeed that is recorded in this book, and what a man he is who experienced it. The only thing to be regretted is that the author of this book, great man as he is, has in recent years grown old and infirm with hoary frost upon his eyebrows.

ACKNOWLEDGEMENTS

The editor and publishers wish to thank the following for permission to use copyright material:

Calder Publications Ltd for an extract from Guillaume Apollinaire, 'Zone' trs. Samuel Beckett from *Collected Poems 1930–78*, Calder (1984);

City Lights Publishers for Frank O'Hara, 'The Day Lady Died' from *Lunch Poems* (1964). © 1964 by Frank O'Hara;

Faber and Faber Ltd for T. S. Eliot, 'Journey of the Magi' from *Collected Poems 1909–1962* and an extract from T. S. Eliot, 'Little Gidding' from *Four Quartets*; an extract from Thom Gunn, 'On the Move' from *Collected Poems*; and with Farrar, Straus & Giroux, Inc. for an extract from Robert Lowell, 'Skunk Hour' from *Life Studies*. © 1956, 1959 by Robert Lowell, renewed © 1987 by Harriet Lowell, Sheridan Lowell and Caroline Lowell;

HarperCollins Publishers for an extract from Hunter S. Thompson, *Fear and Loathing in Las Vegas*, Paladin (1971);

David Higham Associates on behalf of the author for an extract from Charles Nicholl, *The Fruit Palace*, Heinemann (1985); and on behalf of the Estate of the author for Graham Greene, *The Lawless Roads* (1939);

Henry Holt and Company, Inc. for an extract from *Long Lance: The Autobiography of a Blackfoot Indian Chief*. © 1928 by Chief Buffalo Child Long Lance;

Stephen J. Joyce on behalf of the Estate of James Joyce for an extract from James Joyce, *Ulysses*. © The Estate of James Joyce;

Ellen Levine Literary Agency Inc. on behalf of the author for Michael Ondaatje, 'Monsoon Notebook (i)' and 'Monsoon Notebook (ii)' from *Running in the Family*. © 1982 Michael Ondaatje;

CHILDHOOD · FRIENDSHIP · FIRST